The Essential Bu

Royal Enf

BULLE

350, 500 & 535 Singles, 1977-2015

Your marque expert:
Peter Henshaw

Essential Buyer's Guide Series

Alfa Romeo Alfasud – All saloon models from 1971 to 1983 & Sprint models from 1976 to 1989 (Metcalfe)
Alfa Romeo Giulia GT Coupé (Booker)
Alfa Romeo Giulia Spider (Booker)
Audi TT (Davies)
Austin Seven (Barker)
Big Healeys (Trummel)
BMW Boxer Twins – All air-cooled R45, R50, R60, R65, R75, R80, R90, R100, RS, RT & LS (Not GS) models 1969 to 1994 (Henshaw)
BMW E21 3 Series (1975-1983) (Cook & Wylie)
BMW E30 3 Series (1981 to 1994) (Hosier)
BMW GS (Henshaw)
BMW X5 (Saunders)
BSA 350 & 500 Unit Construction Singles (Henshaw)
BSA 500 & 650 Twins (Henshaw)
BSA Bantam (Henshaw)
Citroën 2CV (Paxton)
Citroën ID & DS (Heilig)
Cobra Replicas (Ayre)
Corvette C2 Sting Ray 1963-1967 (Falconer)
Choosing, Using & Maintaining Your Electric Bicycle (Henshaw)
Ducati Bevel Twins (Falloon)
Ducati Desmodue Twins (Falloon)
Ducati Desmoquattro Twins – 851, 888, 916, 996, 998, ST4 1988 to 2004 (Falloon)
Fiat 500 & 600 (Bobbitt)
Ford Capri (Paxton)
Ford Escort Mk1 & Mk2 (Williamson)
Ford Model T – All models 1909 to 1927 (Barker)
Ford Mustang – First Generation 1964 to 1973 (Cook)
Ford Mustang – Fifth generation/S197 (Cook)
Ford RS Cosworth Sierra & Escort (Williamson)
Harley-Davidson Big Twins (Henshaw)
Hillman Imp – All models of the Hillman Imp, Sunbeam Stiletto, Singer Chamois, Hillman Husky & Commer Imp 1963 to 1976 (Morgan)
Hinckley Triumph triples & fours 750, 900, 955, 1000, 1050, 1200 – 1991-2009 (Henshaw)
Honda CBR FireBlade (Henshaw)
Honda CBR600 Hurricane (Henshaw)
Honda SOHC Fours 1969-1984 (Henshaw)
Jaguar E-Type 3.8 & 4.2-litre (Crespin)
Jaguar E-type V12 5.3-litre (Crespin)
Jaguar Mark 1 & 2 (All models including Daimler 2.5-litre V8) 1955 to 1969 (Thorley)
Jaguar S-Type – 1999 to 2007 (Thorley)
Jaguar X-Type – 2001 to 2009 (Thorley)
Jaguar XJ-S (Crespin)
Jaguar XJ6, XJ8 & XJR (Thorley)
Jaguar XK 120, 140 & 150 (Thorley)
Jaguar XK8 & XKR (1996-2005) (Thorley)
Jaguar/Daimler XJ 1994-2003 (Crespin)
Jaguar/Daimler XJ40 (Crespin)
Jaguar/Daimler XJ6, XJ12 & Sovereign (Crespin)
Kawasaki Z1 & Z900 (Orritt)
Land Rover Series I, II & IIA (Thurman)
Land Rover Series III (Thurman)
Lotus Seven replicas & Caterham 7: 1973-2013 (Hawkins)
Mazda MX-5 Miata (Mk1 1989-97 & Mk2 98-2001) (Crook)
Mazda RX-8 All models 2003 to 2012 (Parish)
Mercedes Benz Pagoda 230SL, 250SL & 280SL roadsters & coupès (Bass)
Mercedes-Benz 190 All 190 models (W201 series) 1982 to 1993 (Parish)
Mercedes-Benz 280-560SL & SLC (Bass)
Mercedes-Benz SL R129 Series (Parish)
Mercedes-Benz W123 All models 1976 to 1986 (Parish)
Mercedes-Benz W124 – All models 1984-1997 (Zoporowski)
MG Midget & A-H Sprite (Horler)
MG TD, TF & TF1500 (Jones)
MGA 1955-1962 (Crosier)
MGB & MGB GT (Williams)
MGF & MG TF (Hawkins)
Mini (Paxton)
Morris Minor & 1000 (Newell)
Moto Guzzi 2-valve big twins (Falloon)
New Mini (Collins)
Norton Commando (Henshaw)
Piaggio Scooters – all modern four-stroke automatic models 1991 to 2016 (Willis)
Peugeot 205 GTI (Blackburn)
Porsche 911 (964) (Streather)
Porsche 911 (993) (Streather)
Porsche 911 (996) (Streather)
Porsche 911 (997) Model years 2004 to 2009 (Streather)
Porsche 911 (997) Second generation models 2009 to 2012 (Streather)
Porsche 911 Carrera 3.2 (Streather)
Porsche 911 SC (Streather)
Porsche 924 – All models 1976 to 1988 (Hodgkins)
Porsche 928 (Hemmings)
Porsche 930 Turbo & 911 (930) Turbo (Streather)
Porsche 944 (Higgins)
Porsche 986 Boxster (Streather)
Porsche 987 Boxster & Cayman (Streather)
Rolls-Royce Silver Shadow & Bentley T-Series (Bobbitt)
Royal Enfield Bullet (Henshaw)
Subaru Impreza (Hobbs)
Sunbeam Alpine (Barker)
Triumph 350 & 500 Twins (Henshaw)
Triumph Bonneville (Henshaw)
Triumph Herald & Vitesse (Davies)
Triumph Spitfire & GT6 (Baugues)
Triumph Stag (Mort)
Triumph Thunderbird, Trophy & Tiger (Henshaw)
Triumph TR6 (Williams)
Triumph TR7 & TR8 (Williams)
Velocette 350 & 500 Singles (Henshaw)
Vespa Scooters – Classic two-stroke models 1960-2008 (Paxton)
Volvo 700/900 Series (Beavis)
VW Beetle (Cservenka & Copping)
VW Bus (Cservenka & Copping)
VW Golf GTI (Cservenka & Copping)

www.veloce.co.uk

For post publication news, updates and amendments relating to this book please scan the QR code or visit www.veloce.co.uk/books/V4940

Hubble & Hattie

BATTLE CRY!

First published in September 2016 by Veloce Publishing Limited, Veloce House, Parkway Farm Business Park, Middle Farm Way, Poundbury, Dorchester DT1 3AR, England. Fax 01305 268864 / e-mail info@veloce.co.uk / web www.veloce.co.uk or www.velocebooks.com.
ISBN 978-1-845849-40-5 / UPC 6-36847-04940-9

Readers with ideas for automotive books, or books on other transport or related hobby subjects, are invited to write to the editorial director of Veloce Publishing at the above address. British Library Cataloguing in Publication Data – A catalogue record for this book is available from the British Library. Typesetting, design and page make-up all by Veloce Publishing Ltd on Apple Mac. Printed in India by Replika Press.

Introduction

– the purpose of this book

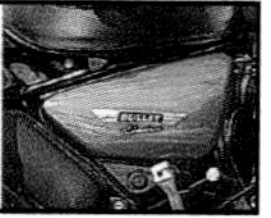

The word 'icon' is overused, but the Royal Enfield Bullet surely deserves to be one. With roots in the early 1950s, it has not only survived into the 21st century, but is now more successful than ever before – in 2015, over 500,000 Bullets were sold in India, where it's now built.

It's an astonishing success story for a bike that some considered obsolete in the early 1960s, when production moved to India from Britain. Since then, the Bullet has changed a great deal, with fuel-injection, disc brakes and a good five-speed gearbox transforming its appeal, though it has stayed faithful to the original concept of a simple air-cooled four-stroke single that is easy to maintain and very economical.

This book is a straightforward, practical guide to buying a Bullet secondhand. It won't list all the correct colour combinations for each year, or analyse the design philosophy – but hopefully it will help you decide whether a Bullet is for you, and if it is, help you avoid buying a dud.

Originally launched in 1948, the Redditch-built Royal Enfield Bullet 350 soon acquired a good reputation – simple, light, compact and with good fuel economy, it was also mechanically strong, relatively oil tight and had the advanced feature

The Bullet has defied obsolescence and survived into the 21st century.

of swingarm rear suspension. Production under licence began in India in 1955, and carried on after Redditch dropped the Bullet in 1962. The bike sold well in India, but exports to Britain didn't start until 1977, with a 350cc kickstart machine that was little changed from the 1950s original.

The incentive for exports, and India's own growing home market, encouraged Enfield to develop the 500cc Bullet, launched in 1988.

The Bullet only began to get some serious development after Enfield was taken over in 1994 by the Eicher Group, one of India's automotive giants. A redesigned engine with alloy barrel arrived in 1999, swiftly followed by electric start, five-speed gearbox and front disc brake.

Most Bullet owners are happy and satisfied – it's a bike that grows on you.

Each of these advances proved very popular, broadening the appeal, and Royal Enfield discovered that many customers wanted a classic style and engine characteristics, with fewer of the hassles associated with old bikes. That was underlined by the arrival of the fuel-injection Bullets in 2009 the retro-styled Classic appealing to the nostalgia market.

Royal Enfield underwent rapid growth from then onwards, mostly on the back of India's burgeoning home market, and production soared to over 100,000 in 2012. The launch of the café racer Continental GT in 2013 brought RE to global attention, and a second factory was built to keep up with demand. Meanwhile, the Bullet remains a good choice secondhand. Although better electrics, braking, the five-speed box and fuel-injection have made the bike more suitable for modern conditions, it remains true to its 1950s roots – it's an easy to own, practical machine that offers a classic riding experience.

This book would not have been possible without the help of several key people: Wayne Olorenshaw at Hitchcocks Motorcycles answered many questions, while Justin Harvey-James and the staff of the Vintage Motorcycle Club allowed me to use the Club's library for research.

Thanks also go to Jacqui Furneaux and Phil Bradshaw, who allowed me to photograph their bikes, and to Vic Ryland of the Royal Enfield Owners' Club.

Contents

The Essential Buyer's Guide™ currency
At the time of publication a BG unit of currency "●" equals approximately £1.00/US$1.33/Euro 1.19. Please adjust to suit current exchange rates using Sterling as the base currency.

1 Is it the right bike for you?
– marriage guidance

Tall and short riders
Good news if you find modern motorcycles too big and heavy. The Bullet is physically small and relatively lightweight, with a seat height of about 750mm. Taller riders don't seem to have a problem with them either.

Running costs
Very low. Although the Bullet isn't the budget bike it used to be, it is cheap to run. All of them give 75-85mpg without extreme economy techniques. Most parts aren't expensive.

Maintenance
Maintenance is a double-edged sword. The Bullet is a simple machine, but it does need more frequent maintenance than a modern bike. Looking after a carburettor Bullet is a case of ongoing maintenance, while service intervals for the EFIs are every 3000km (1800 miles).

Kickstarting
All export market Bullets have had electric start since 2009, but there are still plenty of kickstart bikes around. They aren't difficult by kickstart standards, though the 500 needs more muscle than the 350. That said, it's more about technique than strength.

Usability
Keep off motorways and fast main roads, and Bullets are very usable day-to-day bikes. Fast enough to keep up with urban/suburban traffic, with secure handling. Carburettor bikes are less so, especially the 350 with its weaker front brake.

Parts availability
Could hardly be better, with just about everything available for every model, from Royal Enfield dealers and some very knowledgeable specialists.

Parts costs
Modest, and often cheaper than the equivalent European/Japanese parts, though some later spares, for example: fuel-injection components, aren't cheap.

Insurance group
Bullets are seen as a good risk by insurers, because of the limited performance and often mature, experienced owners. Unless you're using the bike daily, try to find a limited mileage policy to minimise costs.

Investment potential
Limited, simply because the Bullet is now a mass produced motorcycle and there are so many around. The exception is the rare Egli Bullet. A late, very low mileage 350 would be worth hanging onto, as would one of the limited specials produced by Watsonian (see page 18), but even these are unlikely to appreciate.

Foibles
Royal Enfield Bullets respond to sympathetic ownership – look after them on a continuous basis, not just at service intervals, and you should have a reliable machine.

Plus points
Charming 1950s character, combined with (on the later bikes) good brakes, handling and electrics. The antidote to road rage.

Minus points
Limited performance, vibration at high revs, patchy quality on the early bikes, the slow four-speed gearchange and front drum brakes.

Alternatives
There is no direct equivalent to the Bullet (a 1950s design still in production) but any postwar British single will give a similar riding experience, with brakes and electrics from the original era. The retro style with modern (1980s derived) mechanicals are offered by the new generation of 250/400cc singles from China – Mash, Herald, HMC, etc.

Jacqui Furneaux has ridden her Bullet all over the world.

2 Cost considerations

– affordable, or a money pit?

Bullet spares are generally not expensive, and the supply is excellent, with just about everything available. As mentioned elsewhere, these bikes are cheap to run, with fine fuel economy (75-85mpg) and are easy on consumables. The prices quoted here are all from a Royal Enfield spares specialist.

Air cleaner – x7.50
Alternator (pre–1999, 2/3 wires) – x50
Brake shoes (rear, exchange) – x25
Brake shoes (front, exchange) – x25
Battery (12v, kickstart) – x19.50
Cam followers (pr) – x150
Carburettor (Amal conversion) – x150
Clutch plates/spring set – x36
Cylinder barrel (500) – x150
Downpipe – x77
Electronic ignition (Boyer) – x78
Fork springs (pr) – x26
Fork seals (set) – x5
Gasket set – x22
Gearbox sprocket – x36
Headlight glass/reflector – x28
Mudguard (front, stainless steel) – x43
Mudguard (rear, stainless steel) – x59
Oil pump – x22
Chain/sprocket kit – x85
Piston – x65
Primary chain – x37
Rear shocks (Hagon, pr) – x123
Seat – x65
Silencer – x105

Enfields are fuel-efficient and cheap to run.

Speedometer – x35
Valves (UK made) – x25 ea
Wiring loom – x52
Complete restoration (basket case to concours) – around x5000

Well-laden Electra makes a practical tourer.

3 Living with a Bullet

– will you get along together?

In some ways, all of the Bullets are very easy to live with. They were designed from the start as easy to use bikes that anyone could ride, and that still holds true today. Lightweight, physically small and well balanced, they are the ideal choice for anyone who finds a bigger bike intimidating.

However, the 1950s roots do impose a few limitations, especially on the carburettor 350 and 500s. Generally, the later the Bullet, the more modern conveniences it has, which is worth bearing in mind, depending on what blend of old and new you're after.

All Bullets are low powered bikes with an air-cooled long-stroke single-cylinder engine, so performance is sluggish by modern standards. The 350 has a top speed of around 70mph, and a comfortable 50-55mph cruise; the carburettor 500 about 75mph (though with more mid-range torque and more relaxed cruising), while the more powerful fuel-injection bikes can manage 80-85mph and cruise at 60-65mph. None of them were designed for motorways, and cruising a carburettor Bullet flat-out is asking for trouble. Even if nothing goes wrong, the vibration isn't pleasant.

Despite the many updates over the years, those 1950s roots do demand a

Latest EFI is easiest to live with.

degree of mechanical sympathy. It's the sort of mindset that comes naturally to anyone used to riding old bikes, but also applies to the carburettor Bullets and, – to a lesser extent – the EFI machines as well.

Modern bikes just need an engine oil check and chain adjustment between services, but Bullets aren't like that. Maintenance is more of an ongoing process, always keeping an eye open for nuts and bolts coming loose, blown bulbs or tappet adjustment. That's not to say that these things happen all the time, but it's good practice to be on the lookout. It might sound like a chore, but for some people it's one of the attractions of owning a Bullet in the first place. You develop a relationship with it that you don't get with a modern bike that always starts on the button and never goes wrong.

If you don't want to take the classic experience too far, then avoid the carburettor bikes. The four-speed gearbox is slow and agricultural, and the electrics and switchgear are less reliable than on later bikes. The front drum brake on the 350 is weak, and the 500's twin leading-shoe is acceptable as long as it is set up properly, but only the disc-braked Bullets have modern era brakes.

If the thought of cable-operated drum brakes fills you with horror, it's unlikely you'll want to kickstart the bike either. Actually, kickstarting a Bullet is more about technique than leg power, though the 500 does need slightly more muscle than the 350. Both bikes have a decompressor, used to ease the engine over TDC (the ammeter helps here) before the starting kick. In practice, some bikes are easier to start than others, and it takes a while to discover which precise technique works best.

The appearance can be transformed with a few accessories.

So we've established that the Bullet has a starting technique, is not fast, needs considerate ownership and that early brakes, electrics and gearchange aren't up to modern standards. But it's also worth reiterating that this applies to a far lesser extent to the 2009-on fuel–injected Bullets, with their modern conveniences and less intensive maintenance.

You need an element of mechanical sympathy to get along with one of these.

In any case, Bullet ownership has plenty of upsides. Although performance is limited, it's also very relaxed. The pushrod single is low revving, with good mid-range torque, and it's the sort of bike you can put into top gear and leave there. Swooping along a twisty road at 50-60mph is one of the joys of Bullet ownership. They actually handle quite well, despite the staid looks, and reward smooth riding. You can trundle through villages at 30mph and accelerate away with an authentic thump – it's got the feel-good factor in spades.

Bullets also have a practical side. The upside of the low power is that that brake pads/shoes, chains, sprockets and tyres last quite well, so you won't spend a lot on consumables, and the fuel economy is legendary. Keep below 60mph and ride smoothly, and most Bullets should return 75-85mpg, even 90mpg, which is about the same as a 125cc scooter.

They are adaptable bikes, big enough for a passenger – and able to take hard or soft luggage – and even a screen or small fairing, for touring. Package tours of India by Bullet are now a popular holiday choice, and the bikes are perfectly capable of high mileage tours, albeit at a modest pace.

The adaptability extends to customisation, with a huge range of parts available to turn the Bullet into a café racer, a street scrambler, or a trials-style bike. Changing things like the fuel tank, handlebars, seat, exhaust and lights is easy to do, and can transform the looks. And if you really can't live with the performance, there are plenty of options to get more power out of the 500 without compromising reliability.

The bottom line is that Bullets certainly have their limitations, but they are not finicky, difficult-to-live with bikes. Given sympathetic ownership (less crucial on the EFI Bullets) they can offer the simple, unadulterated pleasure of motorcycling as it used to be.

4 Relative values
– which model for you?

Range availability

Four-speed Bullets
Bullet 350 Standard, DL, Superstar, Classic –1977-2008
Bullet 500 Standard, DL, Superstar, Classic – 1988-2008
Bullet 500ES – 2001-2003

Five-speed carburettor Bullets
Bullet Sixty-5 – 2003-2004
Bullet Electra X – 2004-2008

Five-speed fuel-injection Bullets
Electra EFI – 2009 on
Bullet EFI Classic – 2009 on
Bullet EFI B5 – 2011 on
Continental GT 535 – 2013 on
Bullet 350/500 Standard/DL, 500ES

Four-speeds should gradually appreciate in value.

All stated percentage values are in relation to the Sixty-5 & Electra-X models.

The earliest Indian-built Bullets are the closest to the British originals, with a kickstart (apart from the ES), four-speed right-foot gearchange and drum front brake. Unsurprisingly, they give the least modern riding experience and need the most sympathetic ownership, but many are attracted to the classic appeal.

Early four-speed machines give an authentic Brit bike experience.

Of the various models, the 350 Standard is the most classic of all.

Exports began back in 1977, but few were actually sold at first (UK sales were abandoned in the early 1980s, resuming in 1986) and they are now outnumbered on the secondhand market by later 500s. The 350 offers just 17bhp and a cruising speed of 50-55mph, while anything over 60mph brings vibration. The single-leading shoe front drum brake is weak, though many

Five-speed carburettor Bullets are a good compromise between the early four-speeds and the fuel-injection bikes.

bikes will have been upgraded since, and in fact some of these early Indian exports have been fitted with British engines. The same goes for the original 6-volt electrics, as updating to 12-volts is quite straightforward. The 350 is easier to kickstart than the 500 and for many is the 'purest' form of Enfield Bullet.

The 500 launched in 1988 (1990 in the UK), has better mid-range performance, though little more top-end. Higher gearing (a 17-tooth gearbox sprocket) gives more relaxed cruising, though all four-speed bikes have a big ratio gap between third and top. From the start, it had the more powerful 7-inch Twin leading-shoe front brake, though even this needs proper adjustment to work really well. Some bikes suffered from oval brake drums (felt as a pulsing through the lever) which can only be corrected by removing the drum and having it machined round.

All the four-speed Bullets have a slow and notchy gearchange which will come as a mild shock to anyone not used to old bikes. Neutral is difficult to find at a standstill, but uniquely, the box has a neutral finder, a stubby lever located just above the gearchange, that will locate neutral from any gear. The alternative is to slip the bike into neutral just before you roll to a stop.

These early 350/500s come in Standard (black with gold pinstriping and painted mudguards) or Deluxe/ Superstar form (red or black, with chrome on the fuel tank and mudguards).

Electra X: A big step forward, with alloy barrel, more power and front disc brake.

An electric start was optional on the 500 from 2001 (as the Bullet ES) using a Nippon Denso sprag clutch starter. Early sprag clutch bearings and gears can fail if the bike backfires while starting. Later bikes have a spark delay unit which prevents this and can be retro fitted.

Royal Enfield quality has improved over the years, but was most patchy on these early four-speed bikes. Paint, chrome, electrics and brakes could all suffer from variable quality control.

Strengths/weaknesses: Slow gearchange, weak front brake and bullet connector electrics are all downsides. Simplicity and classic appeal are the upsides.

350: 82% 500: 97%

Fuel-injected Bullets are slightly faster than the carb bikes.

Sixty-5 and Electra X

If the 4-speed bikes represent the least developed Bullets, and the fuel-injection machines are the latest, then the Sixty-five and Electra X are a good blend of old and new, still non-unit construction and carburettor, but with some significant steps forward. Announced in 2002, the Sixty-five was touted as the 1960s style Bullet, with its low profile ribbed seat and brighter colours, but the big news was its left-shift five-speed gearbox. Developed in Britain by Stuart McGuigan of Cranfield University, it was a huge advance on the old four-speed box, lighter to use, with an easier to find neutral and with a better spread of closer ratios – fifth gear was the same as the old fourth – which gave improved acceleration. The clutch was also updated with a ball and ramp action. Electric start was standard, but otherwise much was familiar from the existing Bullet 500, with an iron barrel carburettor-fed engine and Twin leading-shoe front drum brake.

This 2012 B5 is a typical low mileage example.

Two years later, the Electra X offered a more comprehensive update. A new version of the air-cooled single was developed in consultation with AVL of Austria, described at the time as Lean

Burn (then a buzz term in the car world for reducing emissions and fuel consumption). The engine was certainly much changed, with higher compression, an alloy cylinder barrel to improve cooling, a rotary oil pump (claimed to be eight times more efficient than the old plunger), roller bearing big-end, electronic ignition and 29mm CV carburettor. Claimed power was up slightly to 23bhp at 5000rpm, and electric start was standard.

B5 is the entry-level Enfield for export markets – styled like the old 350.

There were occasional failures of the roller big-ends (the rollers ran directly in the bearing) but overall the Electra X was a big step forward, and road tests of the time were impressed, judging the bike to feel tighter and built to better tolerances, though not much faster than the old one.

As well as the new engine, the Electra had a 280mm front disc brake, new forks with gaiters and gas shocks – testers were impressed by the disc, but thought the new shocks just as harsh as the old ones. Avon Super Venom tyres were fitted to export bikes.

The Electra's alloy barrel is easy to spot, along with the bigger, more squared–off rocker boxes and the exhaust downpipe secured with two bolts and a flange, rather than a push fit. Side panels and front mudguard were plastic, in the same colour as the tank.

As the road tests pointed out, despite its advances the Electra was little faster than the old 4-speed Bullets, though UK importer Watsonian did offer an optional Highway Kit comprising a 32mm Dell'Orto carburettor and a less restrictive exhaust – this did boost performance, and some bikes may still be fitted with it.

Strengths/weaknesses: Much improved five-speed gearbox, plus front disc and better lubrication on the Electra. Still more maintenance-intensive than the EFI. 100%

Electra, Classic and B5 EFI

Announced in late 2008, the fuel-injected Bullets were the biggest milestone yet. Fuel-injection came partly out of necessity, to meet forthcoming emissions legislation. It was the headline feature in a virtually all-new engine/gearbox of unit construction, wet sump design. A catalyst was added to the exhaust while hydraulic tappets and automatic primary chain tensioner did away with some routine maintenance jobs, and rubber inserts for the cylinder head and barrel fins were designed to reduce noise.

Royal Enfield claimed a significant power boost to 27bhp @ 5250rpm, though performance figures suggest it's not quite that good, with a top speed of around 80-85mph. Fuel consumption is about the same as the carburettor 500s. RE also said the EFI had much lower oil consumption than the carburettor 500, was cheaper to make, and built to tighter tolerances. A new seven-plate clutch was said to be lighter than the old five plate one. Apart from that, mechanical changes were few,

Continental took its inspiration from a 1960s original.

as the Bullet EFI used many parts from the previous five-speed gearbox, and a modified version of the old tubular steel frame.

It was clear that RE used the need for fuel-injection as an opportunity to start from a clean sheet of paper and do what Harley-Davidson did in the 1980s. That is, offer customers a classic looking air-cooled engine that was far quieter, more oil tight and less maintenance-intensive than its predecessor.

Not everyone welcomed EFI, but the Keihin designed system (ECU, throttle body and injector) has proved mostly reliable. The oldest injected bikes are now coming up with minor faults down to corroded connectors, and thanks to tolerances not all the EFIs perform in exactly the same way, but in practice faults are rare. If a major component needs replacing, the parts are expensive by Bullet standards (600 for new ECU and throttle body) and it can be cheaper to replace the system with a Mikuni carburettor, which some owners have done.

At first the Bullet EFI came in Electra or Classic form – the Electra looked very like the old carburettor X, but the new Classic majored on nostalgia, with two-tone paintwork, a solo seat and extra chrome plus rounded rocker boxes. The later Classic Chrome has extra shiny stuff on the tank, mudguards and battery box. An entry-level EFI was added in 2011, the Bullet 500 or B5, which aped the early 350 in style, having valanced mudguards and stepped dual seat. The Satin 500 joined the range in 2012, with a military inspired paint job in matt olive green (Battle Green) or sand (Desert Storm).

Strengths/weaknesses: Slightly more power, less maintenance, more oil-tight, fewer emissions. Electronic fuel-injection parts expensive, and the complexity is at odds with the Bullet ethos of simplicity.
150%

Continental GT 535

The Continental GT was a major departure for Royal Enfield, signalling its intention to broaden its range of bikes and become the world's leading manufacturer in the 250-750cc class.

Although it harked back to Royal Enfield's original Continental GT of 1965, much of the modern version was new. A new frame was designed by Harris Racing of Britain (later taken in-house by RE to focus on R&D) and the bike was designed by British design house Xenophya. It certainly looked the part of a modern retro café racer, and the sporty looks were backed up by quality European components – Brembo discs front and rear, Paioli gas shocks and Pirelli Sport Demon tyres on Excel rims. Gone was the old Bullet nacelle and in came a separate chrome headlight with matching speedometer and rev counter. Mildly rearset footrests, clip-on style bars and solo seat were finishing touches.

But although the new GT looked the part and had an impressive list of

The GT doesn't offer much more power than standard Bullets, but certainly looks the part, and tuning parts are available.

equipment, it's engine was only mildly upgraded from the standard 500 EFI. Capacity was boosted to 535cc, it had a larger throttle body and a lighter crank, the latter to enable revs to build faster. So RE claimed only a modest power boost to 29bhp @ 5100rpm, and rolling road tests suggested that even that was optimistic. As a result, although acceleration is better than the standard EFI, top speed is about the same.

But none of that seems to have mattered to the buyers, and the GT has been a hit, both with older riders in export markets seeking to relive their youth, as well as younger Indians. According to UK spares specialist Hitchcocks, it's quite easy to boost the GT's power, with bigger valves, hotter cams and a Power Commander to remap the ECU. As the GT has been a good seller, there is plenty of choice secondhand.

Strengths/weaknesses: Fine handling, good braking and spot-on looks. Standard GT lacks performance, but tuning parts are readily available.
168%

Diesel Bullets

There aren't many diesel motorcycles in the world, but there are more diesel Bullets than anything else, and the reason isn't hard to find. As the only new motorcycle of the 1990s and 2000s with a separate engine and gearbox, the Bullet was relatively easy to convert to diesel power – a single-cylinder diesel of 3-500cc, commonly

Well–used Enfield Robin Diesel: one of the first built.

Diesel Bullets give a relaxed ride, and extreme fuel economy.

used as stationary power units for generators and water pumps, could be bolted in to replace the standard engine.

Royal Enfield produced its own diesel Bullet from 1993, a 325cc which mustered just 6bhp and claimed fuel consumption of 202mpg, but this has never been officially exported to the West.

In Europe, a few conversions have been available since 1993, notably the Enfield Robin (converted in the UK using a 412cc Fuji Industries engine) and the Sommer, a German conversion using a 462cc Hatz unit, and still available new in 2016. That year, Price Part Motorcycles was still offering its own conversion in the UK, with a Yanmar clone diesel.

All diesel Enfields offer slower acceleration than a 350 Bullet, but a similar cruising speed, and of course they are very economical. The author's Enfield Robin has always returned 170-190mpg.

Strengths/Weaknesses: Uniqueness and interest factor, extreme economy and mechanical simplicity, but very slow.

Specials

As mentioned on page 11, one of the attractions of the Bullet is that it is easily customisable by simply swapping some key parts such as exhaust, seat, tank, etc.

Watsonian-Squire, the UK importer until 2012, took advantage of this by offering a series of UK-only specials, all of them cosmetic variations on the standard Bullet. The Clubman was a forerunner of today's Continental GT, with a big alloy fuel tank, humped solo seat and swept back exhaust. The Woodsman had a slightly off-road look, with high-level pipe and solo seat, and there were more serious looking T350 and 500 trials bikes as well, suitable for green laning. The Sixty-Five Street was a street scrambler, while the XS and XR were sportier variants of the Electra X – with rev counter, Avon Super Venom tyres and chrome mudguards. In the UK, the Clubman is the most common Watsonian special to turn up secondhand.

Enfield spares specialist, Hitchcocks Motorcycles doesn't offer complete specials in the way that Watsonian did, instead having a vast catalogue of parts from which customers can choose. Most striking are the Rigid Enfield (which replaces the standard swingarm with a rigid rear), the Continental (an alloy take on

Well before the factory GT, UK importer Watsonian was offering the Clubman.

the café racer) and the trials. There is no common specification for these bikes, but all spares are available through Hitchcocks.

Finally, in the 1990s, renowned Swiss frame builder Fritz Egli offered the Super Bullet, a 624cc conversion aimed at producing serious performance. These are very rare, so expect to pay more if you find one.
160%

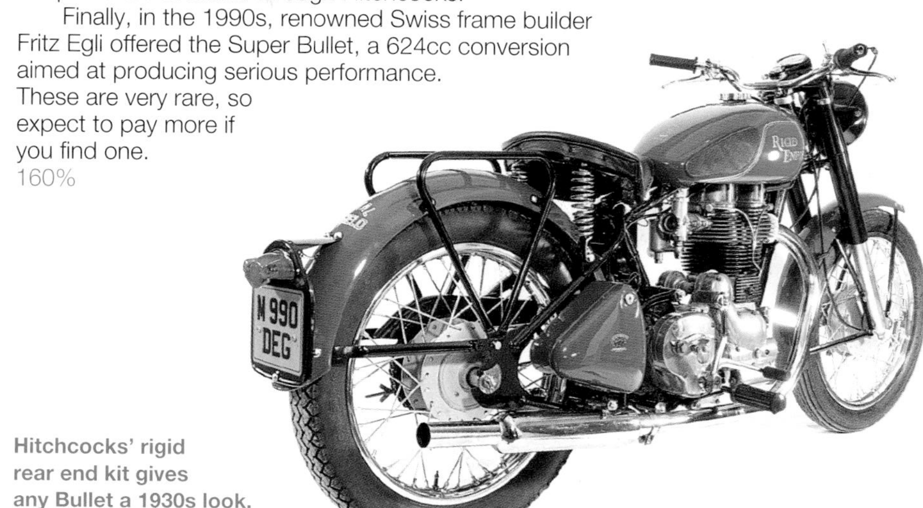

Hitchcocks' rigid rear end kit gives any Bullet a 1930s look.

5 Before you view
– be well informed

To avoid a wasted journey, and the disappointment of finding that the bike does not match your expectations, it will help if you're very clear about what questions you want to ask before you pick up the phone. Some of these points might appear basic, but when you're excited about the prospect of buying your dream bike, it's amazing how some of the most obvious things slip the mind... Also check the current values of the model you are interested in the classic bike magazine classified ads and online.

Where is the bike?
Is it going to be worth travelling to the next county/state, or even across a border? A locally advertised machine, although it may not sound very interesting, can add to your knowledge for very little effort, so make a visit – it might even be in better condition than expected.

Dealer or private sale
Establish early on if the bike is being sold by its owner or by a trader. A private owner should have all the history, so don't be afraid to ask detailed questions. A dealer may have more limited knowledge of the bike's history, but should have some documentation. A dealer may offer a warranty/guarantee (ask for a printed copy).

Cost of collection and delivery
A dealer may well be used to quoting for delivery. A private owner may agree to meet you halfway, but only agree to this after you have seen the bike at the vendor's address to validate the documents. Conversely, you could meet halfway and agree the sale, but insist on meeting at the vendor's address for the handover.

View - when and where
It is always preferable to view at the vendor's home or business premises. In the case of a private sale, the bike's documentation should tally with the vendor's name and address. Arrange to view only in daylight, and avoid a wet day – the vendor may be reluctant to let you take a test ride if it's wet.

Reason for sale
Do make it one of the first questions. Why is the bike being sold and how long has it been with the current owner? How many previous owners?

Condition
Ask for an honest appraisal of the bike's condition. Ask specifically about some of the check items described in Chapter 7.

All original specification
As the Bullet is still in production, it's less collectable, and a completely original specification is less critical than for a genuine classic. A four-speed 350 or 500 which is just as it left the factory is more desirable than one.

Matching data/legal ownership

Do frame, engine numbers and licence plate match the official registration document? Is the owner's name and address recorded in the official registration documents?

For those countries that require an annual test of roadworthiness, does the bike have a document showing it complies? (an MoT certificate in the UK, which can be verified on 0845 600 5977).

In the UK, bikes registered in 1976 or earlier are exempt from VED (Vehicle Excise Duty, better known as 'road tax') but this does not apply to any Indian-made Bullets, apart from the odd pre-1974 personal import.

Does the vendor own the bike outright? Money might be owed to a finance company or bank: the bike could even be stolen. Several organisations will supply the data on ownership, based on the bike's licence plate number, for a fee. Such companies can often also tell you whether the bike has been 'written-off' by an insurance company. In the UK these organisations can supply vehicle data:

HPI – 01722 422 422 – www.hpicheck.com
AA – 0870 600 0836 – www.theaa.com
RAC – 0870 533 3660 – www.rac.co.uk

Other countries will have similar organisations.

Unleaded fuel

All Indian-made Bullets will run happily on unleaded fuel.

Insurance

Check with your existing insurer before setting out – your current policy might not cover you if you do buy the bike and decide to ride it home.

How you can pay

A cheque/check will take several days to clear and the seller may prefer to sell to a cash buyer. However, a banker's draft (a cheque issued by a bank) is as good as cash, but safer, so contact your own bank and become familiar with the formalities that are necessary to obtain one. Paying by electronic transfer via internet banking is the quickest means of all.

Buying at auction?

If the intention is to buy at auction, see Chapter 10 for further advice.

Professional vehicle check (mechanical examination)

There are often marque/model specialists who will undertake professional examination of a vehicle on your behalf. Owners clubs may be able to put you in touch with such specialists.

6 Inspection equipment

– these items will really help

This book

Before you rush out of the door, gather together a few items that will help as you work your way around the bike. This book is designed to be your guide at every step, so take it along and use the check boxes to help you assess each area of the bike you're interested in. Don't be afraid to let the seller see you using it.

Reading glasses (if you need them for close work)

Take your reading glasses if you need them to read documents and make close-up inspections.

Overalls/camera/smartphone

Be prepared to get dirty. Take along a pair of overalls, if you have them, and a camera or smartphone, so that later you can study some areas of the bike more closely. Take a picture of any part of the bike that causes you concern, and seek a friend's opinion.

Compression tester

A compression tester is easy to use. It screws into the sparkplug hole, and on a Bullet this couldn't be easier to get to. With the ignition off, turn the engine over on full throttle to get the compression reading.

A friend, preferably a knowledgeable enthusiast

Ideally, have a friend or knowledgeable enthusiast accompany you: a second opinion is always valuable.

7 Fifteen minute evaluation
– walk away or stay?

Engine/frame numbers

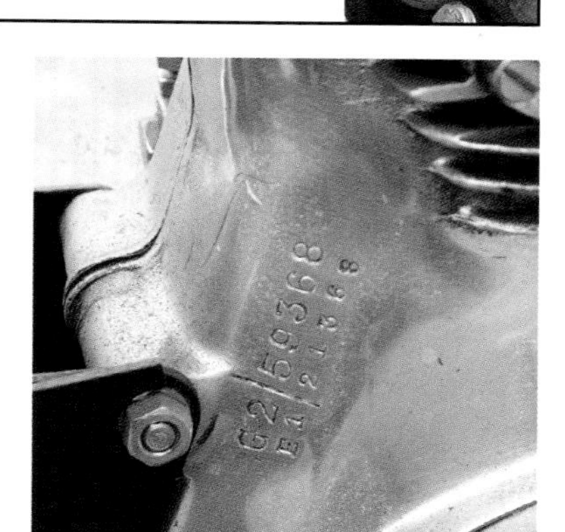
Engine number gives a clue to the bike's type and age.

Engine and frame numbers are mentioned several times in this book, with good reason. They are unique to the bike; a means of checking whether the documentation relates to the bike, and whether the engine and frame are original. Unlike some older British bikes, the engine and frame numbers were not matching when the bike was new.

Check the engine number – on the left-hand front of the crankcase on carburettor Bullets, left-hand rear on EFIs – and the frame number, on the right-hand side of the headstock on all bikes. The frame number may be difficult to decipher if the frame has been repainted, but it is there. Efi Bullets also have a VIN plate, found on the frame downtube. Any 'fuzzy' numbers could be a sign of tampering.

Documentation

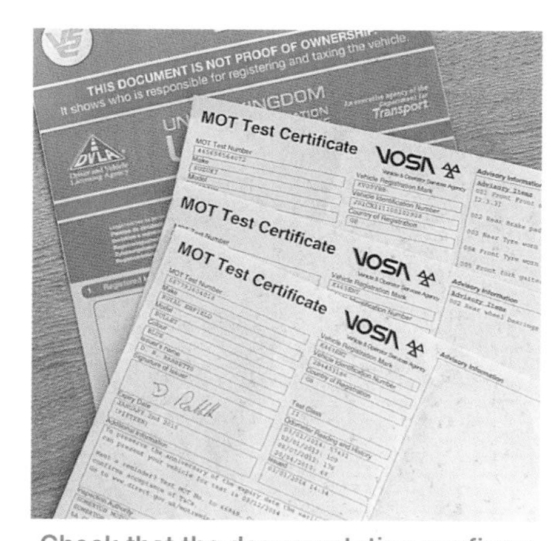

Check that the documentation confirms the bike's provenance.

If the seller claims to be the bike's owner, make sure he/she really is by checking the registration document, which in the UK is V5C. The person listed on the V5C isn't necessarily the legal owner, but their details should match those of whoever is selling the bike. Also check that the engine/frame numbers on the V5C are the same as those on the bike.

An annual roadworthiness certificate – the 'MoT' in the UK – is handy proof not just that the bike was roadworthy when tested, but if there's a whole sheaf of them, gives evidence of the bike's history – when it was actively being used, and what the mileage was. The more of these that come with the bike, the better.

Beware non-export bikes

Royal Enfield built specific versions of the Bullet for export, with a better finish; but some Indian home market bikes do turn up for sale in other countries. These will be personal imports, and a few have even been ridden overland to Europe.

Official export Bullets have details like polished alloy, lacquered paintwork, stainless steel spokes and nicely rolled edges to the mudguards. Home market bikes don't have any of this. A front number plate is another giveaway of an Indian bike. Certain models have never been officially exported to Europe – the Thunderbird, Lightning and Machismo, for example, have never been officially available in the UK. One of these might be worth buying for its rarity value outside India though.

Some bikes are hybrids – Indian Bullets that have been fitted with British engines, and vice versa. Beware of 500cc Bullets claimed to be from the 1960s or '70s – the 500 wasn't launched until 1988. Finally, it's not unknown for sellers of Indian Bullets to try and pass them off as more valuable British-built bikes. Engine numbers G2 66XXX EI XXXXX onwards have Indian made crankcases.

Indian registration is a giveaway that this bike is a personal import.

General condition

Put the bike on its centre stand, to shed equal light on both sides, and take a good, slow walk around it. If it's claimed to be restored, and has a nice shiny tank and engine cases, look more closely – how far does the 'restored' finish go? Are the nooks and crannies behind the gearbox as spotless as the fuel tank? If not, the bike may have been given a quick smarten up to sell. A generally faded look all over isn't necessarily a bad thing – it suggests a machine that hasn't been restored, and isn't trying to pretend that it has.

Now look at the engine – the most expensive and time-consuming thing to put right if anything's wrong. A light misting of oil here and there is nothing to worry about, most commonly from the head gasket on carburettor Bullets, but still not inevitable. If the rear of the bike looks oily, it could be just oil forced out of the breather, though this is a sign that the bike has been ridden hard.

Put the bike on its centre stand and take a slow walk around it.

Take the bike off the centre stand and start the engine – a kickstart bike should fire up within two or three kicks, and rev up crisply and cleanly without showing blue or black smoke. Some top end tapping is normal, but listen for rumbles and knocks from the bottom end. While the engine's running, check that the ignition light or ammeter show the electrics are charging.

Switch off the engine and put the bike back on its centre stand. Check for play in the forks, headstock and swingarm. Are there leaks from the forks or rear shocks?

8 Key points
– where to look for problems

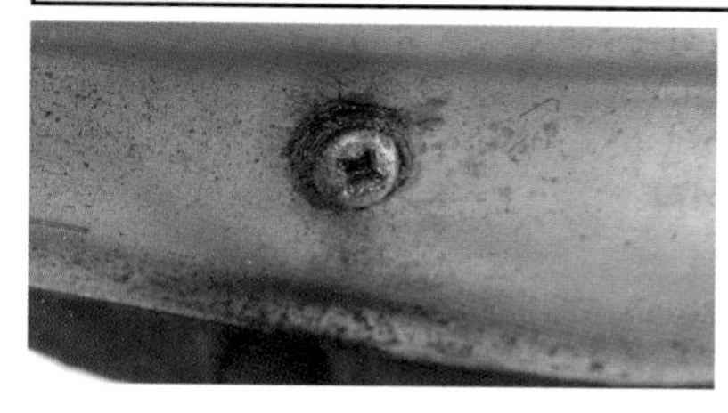

Are the bolt or screw heads chewed or rounded-off? Is there damage to casings around bolt heads? Has someone attacked fixings with a hammer and chisel? All are sure signs of a careless previous owner with more enthusiasm than skill, coupled with a dash of impatience. Not a good sign.

A high mileage should be reflected in the price – most Bullets don't cover many miles per year.

The frame number is on the right-hand side of the steering head. A repainted frame may make it difficult to decipher, or, as in this case, totally illegible!

Listen to the engine running. Clonks or rumbles from the bottom end indicate that the main or big-end bearings are worn. Any blue smoke may suggest a worn top end – that means valves and valve guides, the piston, rings and cylinder bore.

On electric start Bullets, does the starter engage? If it doesn't, the sprag clutch has failed.

9 Serious evaluation

– 30 minutes for years of enjoyment

Circle the Excellent, Good, Average or Poor box of each section as you go along. The totting up procedure is detailed at the end of the chapter. Be realistic in your marking!

Engine/frame numbers

The engine and frame numbers should be the first thing to examine and compare to the registration document. They're not an infallible guide to originality, as some early Bullets will have had replacement engines and/or frames over their long lives. For example, some early Indian bikes have had British Bullet engines fitted – both these and early Indian Bullet 350s have a G2 prefix. An EI in the number confirms that the engine was built in India.

On carburettor bikes, the engine number is located on the front of the left-hand crankcase. The engine number's first digit shows the year ('3' signifies 1983, '93 or 2003!) and the second is B for Bullet. The third represents variations: '5' for 500 (350s don't have a number), 'S' for electric start, 'F' for five-speed). Next is the engine's individual serial number, and finally there's a lettter showing the month of production – A for January, and so on, though I and J are not used. eg: 3-B-53000B is a 1983, 93 or 03 Bullet 500, no. 3000 made in Feb. If the number looks as if it's been tampered with, or doesn't tally with the paperwork, then beware.

Now look for the frame number, on the right-hand side of the head stock. This may be difficult to decipher, especially if the frame has been repainted, but it is there!

Frame number is on the right-hand side of the head stock.

Fuel-injection bikes have a VIN plate riveted to the frame ...

... and an engine number on top of the crankcase.

Fuel injected Bullets also have a VIN plate, riveted to the frame downtube. All EFI engine numbers are stamped on the top of the left-hand side of the crankcase, just behind the starter motor. Check that these tally with those on the registration document. Wherever the number is, if it doesn't tally with the paperwork, walk away.

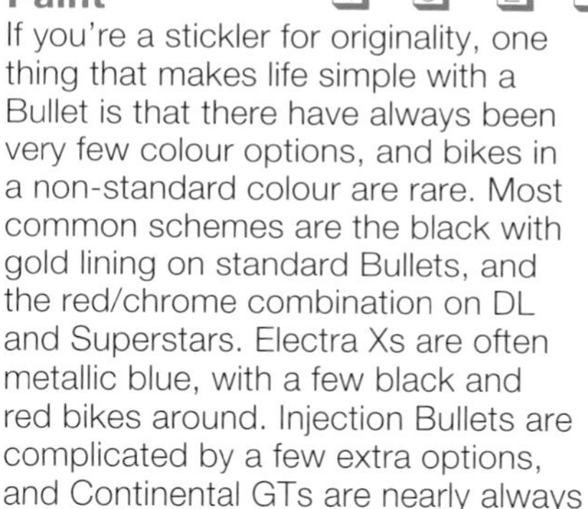

Paint 4 3 2 1

If you're a stickler for originality, one thing that makes life simple with a Bullet is that there have always been very few colour options, and bikes in a non-standard colour are rare. Most common schemes are the black with gold lining on standard Bullets, and the red/chrome combination on DL and Superstars. Electra Xs are often metallic blue, with a few black and red bikes around. Injection Bullets are complicated by a few extra options, and Continental GTs are nearly always bright red!

Early Indian Enfield quality was not good, and this extended to the paintwork, which could be patchy and dull. It has improved dramatically over the years, but even EFI Bullets are not immune to paint faults, which can allow rust to bubble up from underneath. Continental GTs assembled and painted in a brand new factory have the best quality paintwork of all. On a Satin, check that the matt finish has not gone patchy.

Few Indian Enfields appear to have been repainted, perhaps thanks to their lower value and less exotic image compared to older British classics. Look for evidence of quick and cheap resprays, with wobbly pinstriping, for example. Light staining around the filler cap, from spilt fuel, should polish out, but might require a respray. Generally faded original paintwork isn't necessarily a bad thing, and some riders even prefer this original and unrestored look.

Continental GT, built in a new factory, has better paint finish.

Paint quality varies on earlier Bullets, but this one should polish up well.

Sixty-5 onwards used plastic side panels.

Tinwork 4 3 2 1

Nacelles last well.

In one respect, buying a secondhand bike is far easier than purchasing a used car – there's far less bodywork to worry about – especially the Bullet, which has always been sold with the bare minimum of tinwork – fuel tank, mudguards and side panels, and some of these are plastic on later bikes. Plus the lovely headlight nacelle, something of a Bullet trademark and fitted to every bike except the GT, Superstar and a few specials. The good news is that everything is available as a new spare.

The mudguard stays are prone to fracture, especially on the deeper, heavier guards fitted to the standard 350/500 Bullets and the EFI B5, so check these are secure. Mudguards themselves should be straight, free of rust around the rims and securely bolted to the bike. GTs have plastic mudguards.

The fuel tank needs to be checked for leaks around the tap and along the seams, as well as dents and rust. Watch out for patches of filler. Repairing leaks means flushing it out (which has to be thorough – you don't want any petrol vapour hanging about when the welding torch is fired up) but the fuel tank is at least easy to remove via four bolts. Pinhole leaks can often be cured by Petseal, but anything more serious needs a proper repair. If the tank is beyond saving, new ones are available for both carburettor and EFI bikes. The new tank might also need painting, but either way this isn't a cheap option, making a very poor condition tank a good bargaining lever.

The nacelle doesn't appear to be prone to rust, as it's a pretty solid item.

Metal toolbox on four-speed bikes.

Check fuel tank for leaks and dents.

Chrome 4 3 2 1

Early chrome was prone to rust and flaking.

The Bullet is a classic looking bike, and good chrome is central to its appeal, especially the DL, Superstar and Classic Chrome. Unfortunately, the early chrome plating was of poor quality, and that on the wheel rims, exhaust and bars will all rust if not kept clean. It may even flake off the rims, something which happened to the author's 1993 Bullet.

Whichever bike you're looking at, check the chrome for rust, pitting and general dullness. Minor blemishes can be polished away, but otherwise you're looking at a replating bill. If the silencers are seriously rotted, it's a better idea to budget for a new pair – less hassle than getting the old ones replated in any case. Alloy rims and stainless steel spokes are a popular choice to replace flaky/rusty rims – not cheap, but you'll never be bothered by rust again.

Seat

  2 

A variety of seats are fitted to the Bullet; the most common being the stepped type, fitted to all early bikes (pre-Sixty-5) and the B5. The Sixty-5 had a flatter ribbed seat, and many Classics and Satins have solo seats, which are a popular aftermarket fitment for Bullets. The GT has its own humped solo seat and although a dual seat is optional, most owners stick with the solo for a more authentic café racer look.

Whichever seat the bike has, the points to look for are the same. The metal pan can rust, which will eventually give way, though this is easy to check. Covers can split, which of course allows the rain in, which the foam padding soaks up ... and it never dries out. That's a recipe for a permanently wet backside, or a rock hard seat on frosty mornings (the author speaks from experience). New covers and complete seats in a variety of styles are available, although re-covering an old seat is a specialist job.

Twin solo seats are rare.

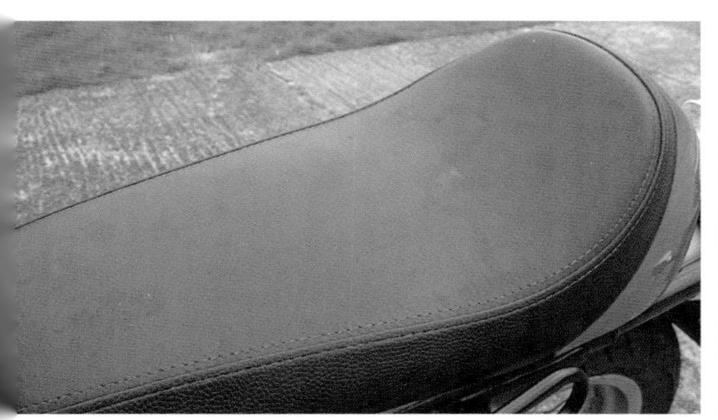

GT has a humped solo seat; some owners fit the dual seat.

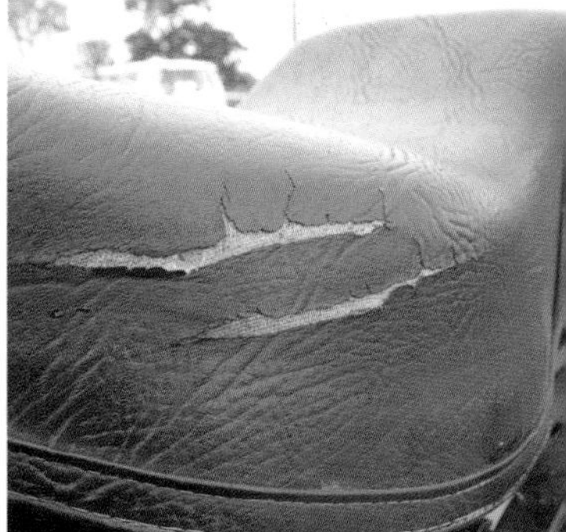

Split seats soon let in water.

Footrest /kickstart rubbers

Worn footrest rubbers are a good sign of high mileage, though as they're so cheap and easy to replace, not an infallible one. They should be secure on the footrest and free of splits or tears. If the footrest itself is bent upwards, that's a sure sign the bike has been down the road at some point, so look for other tell-tale signs on that side. The kickstart and gearchange rubbers are also easy to replace, so well worn ones could indicate owner neglect.

On kickstart bikes, beware the worn smooth rubber – your foot's liable to slip off while kicking the bike over, with painful results as the kickstart lever slams back into your leg.

Well worn footrest rubber.

Left-foot gearchange rubber.

The rubber should also be firm on the lever and not drop off after half a dozen kicks. Of course, if the engine needs that many kicks to fire it up, then something's wrong there anyway.

Frame

4 3 2 1

Royal Enfield may have pioneered the swingarm frame, but that was in the late 1940s. All Bullets except the GT have stuck with basically the same simple design of tubular steel, single downtube frame. Despite the many changes that have been made to the bike's running gear, the frame has only changed slightly over the years. Diesel engined Bullets will usually have had radical modifications to the frame, so check this has been done properly. EFIs, Electras and Classics use the same single downtube frame, but with detail differences on things like footrest and seat mountings. The GT has its own frame with twin downtubes, designed by Harris Racing.

EFI uses a modified version of the earlier frame.

All bikes have a swingarm pivoting on metalastic bonded rubber bushes (nylon bushes on the EFI) which do not need lubrication, and can be replaced if need be.

Whichever frame it is, the most important job is to check that it's straight and true. Crash damage may have bent it, putting the wheels out of line. One way to check is by experienced eye, string and a straight edge, but the surest way to ascertain a frame's straightness is on the test ride – any serious misalignment should be obvious in the way the bike handles.

A frame that is really shabby necessitates a strip down and repaint, though as with the other

Modified single downtube on an Enfield Robin.

paintwork, if it's original and fits in with the patina of the bike, then there's a good case for leaving it as it is.

Look for bent brackets, which can be heated and bent back into shape, and cracks around them, which can be welded.

Twin downtube frame on the GT.

Stands

4 3 2 1

Every Bullet has a centre stand, which is very useful for chain maintenance, and most have a sidestand as well – well worth having, too, as hauling a Bullet onto its centre stand every time you park can become a bit of a pain. The centre stand is made of steel, as opposed to cast alloy on the British-made Bullets, and seems to be strong enough.

Both stands should be secure. When on the centre stand, the bike shouldn't wobble or lean, a sign of serious stand wear and/or imminent collapse. If previous owners have been in the habit of running the bike on its stand, that won't help.

Later sidestands are sturdy.

Check the centre stand is secure.

Lights

4 3 2 1

Bullet lights were upgraded from 6 volts to 12 in 1986, although by now it's likely that most early bikes will have been converted to 12 volts in any case. Whatever the age, look for a tarnished or rusted reflector, which is an MoT failure; though reflectors, bulbs, glass and headlight shells are all available. Also, check that the headlight pilot light, and the neat little running lights set into the nacelle, are all working – these little bulbs can blow, but LED replacements are readily available.

Headlights improved over the years.

Various styles of rear light have been fitted, and all are available as spares, plus a good selection of aftermarket lights if you want your bike to look different. One modification that doesn't alter the outward appearance is an LED rear/stop light bulb. This is a straight swap for the standard bulb, but won't blow, leaving you taillight-less on a dark night.

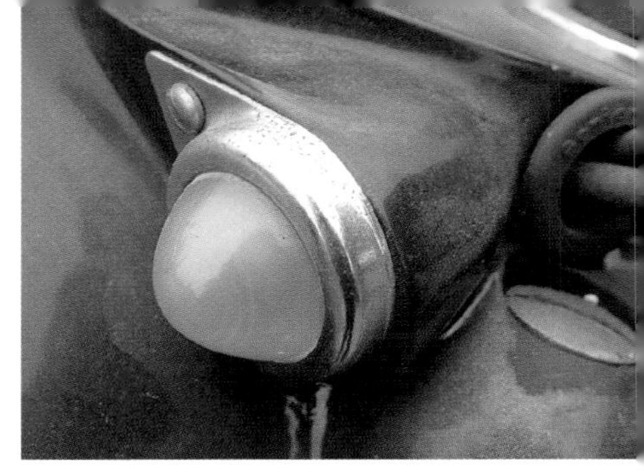
Running lights – a Bullet trademark – do they work?

Electrics/wiring 4 3 2 1

The Bullet's electrics are basically sound, but, like any system, depend on the quality of the connections (especially earths) to be reliable. So check that everything works: lights, indicators, horn and starter. The most common fault is a poor earth at the battery, though the clearance of the battery box over the terminals on early bikes is very tight, which can lead to shorting out. Poor earthing of the rear/stop light circuit can also cause problems.

Pre-1986 6-volt_systems can be made reliable. They used an alternator and rectifier, with regulation through the light switch, which can fail. For modern use, conversion to 12 volts is a good idea, and many bikes will have had this done already – if so, ask who did the conversion.

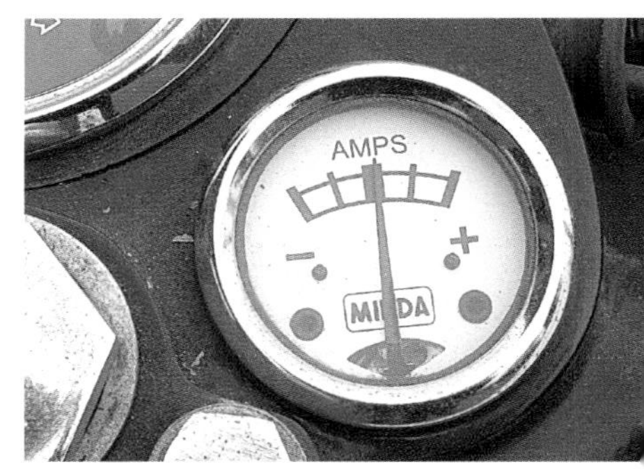

Ammeter, standard on all carburettor Bullets, is a handy instrument.

Block connectors replaced the old-style bullet connectors in 1998, and the following year saw 12-volt DC electrics (replacing AC/DC) with a four-wire alternator (two wires to the headlight, two to the rest of the system) – the previous alternator had two or three wires. Electronic ignition arrived with the Electra in 2004, but can be retro fitted to any bike – the Boyer system, which replaces the cb points, condensor and advance unit, is a popular choice.

Even if sensible modifications have been done, the electrical system still needs checking. A good general indication of the owner's attitude is the condition of the wiring – is it tidy and neat, or flopping around?

The many bullet connectors on pre-'98 bikes need to be clean and tight, and many odd electrical problems are simply down to bad connections or a poor earth. This applies to the EFIs just

State of wiring gives a clue to the rest of the electrics.

as much as the earlier bikes, and in fact good connections are even more vital, as the ECU is sensitive to unreliable signals.

One advantage of carburettor Bullets is that all of them have an ammeter as standard, so you can instantly check whether the system is charging – it should be charging with the lights on, on a fast idle.

All connectors should be clean and tight.

Wheels/tyres 4 3 2 1

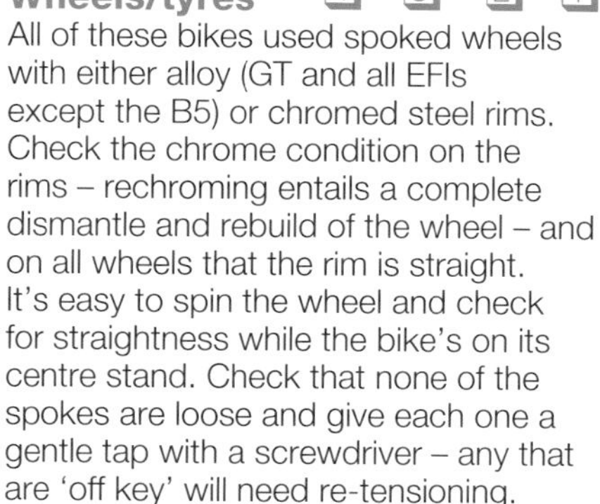

All of these bikes used spoked wheels with either alloy (GT and all EFIs except the B5) or chromed steel rims. Check the chrome condition on the rims – rechroming entails a complete dismantle and rebuild of the wheel – and on all wheels that the rim is straight. It's easy to spin the wheel and check for straightness while the bike's on its centre stand. Check that none of the spokes are loose and give each one a gentle tap with a screwdriver – any that are 'off key' will need re-tensioning.

Tyres should have at least the legal minimum of tread. In the UK that's at least 1mm of tread depth across at least three-quarters of the breadth of the tyre. Or if the tread doesn't reach that far across the breadth (true of some modern tyres) then any tread showing must be at least 1mm deep. Beware of bikes that have been left standing (especially on the sidestand) for some

Worn tyres are a good bargaining lever, though this one is almost new.

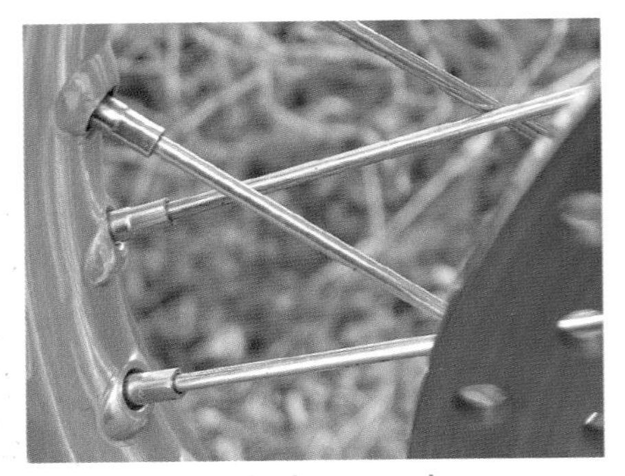

Check for loose spokes.

time, allowing the tyres to crack and deteriorate – it's no reason to reject the bike, but a good lever to reduce the price. New tyres in suitable sizes are no problem at all, and modern grippy tyres can be fitted to older bikes.

Avon SM rear is found on many Bullets, but more modern equivalents will fit.

Wheel bearings

4 3 2 1

Wheel bearings aren't expensive, but fitting them is a hassle, and if there's play it could affect the handling. To check them, put the bike on its centre stand, put the steering on full lock and try rocking the front wheel in a vertical plane, then spin the wheel and listen for signs of roughness. Do the same for the rear wheel. If they do need replacing, try to find sealed replacements, which will last longer.

Steering head bearings

4 3 2 1

Again, the bearings don't cost an arm or leg, but trouble here can affect the handling, and changing them is a big job. With the bike on the centre stand swing the handlebars from lock to lock. They should move freely, with not a hint of

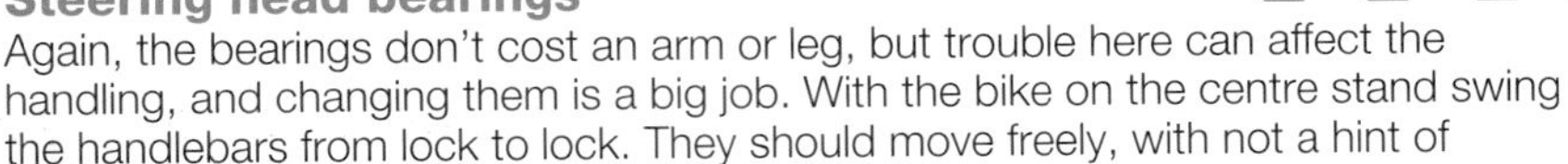

Any play here means a wheel bearing change.

Don't forget steering head bearings.

roughness or stiff patches – if there is, budget for replacing them. To check for play, put the front brake on hard and attempt to rock the bike gently back and forth.

Swingarm bearings

4 3 2 1

Another essential for good handling is the swingarm bearings. The silent bloc-bonded rubber bushes don't need greasing (ditto the nylon bearings on EFIs), but they will deteriorate after a while, in which case, they will need replacing. To check for wear, get hold of the rear wheel and try rocking the complete swingarm from side to side, feeling for any movement at the pivot. There should be nothing perceptible, but if there is, haggle on the price, as replacement is a difficult job.

There should be no side play in the swingarm.

Suspension

4 3 2 1

The Bullet's suspension reflects the era it comes out of – non-adjustable telescopic front forks (shrouded or gaitered) and pre-load adjustable twin rear shocks. The forks didn't really change until the Electra, which adopted alloy bottom sliders incorporating a bracket casting for a disc brake, but kept the distinctive 'leading-linking' spindle mounting. The EFI changed to a conventional spindle mounting and the Classics had different mudguard mountings to the other bikes, with shrouded forks. GTs have exposed forks and Paioli gas shocks.

Check the forks and rear shocks for leaks. The fork stanchions' chrome plate eventually pits, especially if exposed to the elements and/or the bike has been

Despite their 1950s roots, shrouded forks don't give much trouble.

Leaking shocks or loss of damping will mean replacement.

Exposed stanchions on a GT should be kept clean.

used in winter. When that happens, it rapidly destroys the oil seals – hence the leaks. New stanchions, or reground and re-plated existing ones, are the answer, as there's little point in fitting new seals to rough forks. The shocks are easy to check for leaks, but if the forks have gaiters, try rubbing the gaiter against the stanchion inside it. If it moves very easily, then there's likely to be a leak. Also check the forks' spindle mounting castings, which can crack if overtightened.

Check for play by gripping the bottom of the forks and trying to rock them back and forth; play here indicates worn bushes. Worn out rear shocks will manifest a high speed weave, and sick forks will likewise spoil the bike's handling.

Nice matching clocks on the GT.

1993 Bullet instruments, with later replacement speedo – and accessory clock.

Instruments   

Instrumention is basic, though all carburettor Bullets have an ammeter as well as the speedo – EFIs have a warning light cluster instead. Early bikes had km/h speedos, which means the odometer is in kilometres, too. The GT has an attractive matching speedo/rev counter, aping British bikes of the 1960s.

Checking the speedo works obviously has to wait for the test ride – if nothing is working, the cable is the most likely culprit, though if either the odometer or speedo has ceased to function, but the other is still working, then there's something wrong internally – instrument repair is best left to a specialist. They do wear out eventually (the speedos, not the specialists) but new ones are available. A battered and bent chrome bezel suggests that a previous owner has had a go themselves.

Engine/gearbox – general impression   

Enfield Bullet engines are simple, and in some ways, easy to work on, although over the years this does encourage some keen owners to take things apart, sometimes without the proper tools or knowledge. So look for chewed up screw or allen bolt heads and rounded–off bolts, plus damage to the casings surrounding them.

Check for oil leaks. By British bike standards, the Bullets were quite oil tight, and the same holds true of the Indian Enfields. Misting around the primary drive cover is common, and head gaskets can leak on carburettor bikes (though torquing the cylinder head down will help). EFIs may have a weep from the starter motor cover, which has no gasket. A drip on the left, towards the rear of the gearbox, is likely to be the gearbox sprocket – replacing that seal means taking the clutch out. All bikes will blow oil out of the breather (which exits into the air filter box) if ridden hard, so what looks like a leak from below the filter box could be just that. Oil will also be forced out if the bike is overfilled (it should be halfway up the dipstick, not on the max mark). Carburettor bikes can suffer from wet sumping – oil draining from the tank into the crankcase – if they are left unused for long periods.

Many of the same comments apply to the gearbox – look for chewed fasteners and signs of neglect. Remove the oil filler cap and stick a finger inside to check whether the oil has been changed recently – nice clean EP90 ... or a frothy sludge. Grease is recommended for four-speed boxes, but many owners use oil anyway.

Air-cooled Bullet single is mechanically noisier than a modern water-cooled engine.

Engine – starting/idling

4 3 2 1

On kickstart bikes, ask the owner to start it. He/she should have the right technique worked out, and if they can't start it within two or three kicks, then something's wrong. The 350s are quite easy to kick into life and though 500s need a bit more muscle, technique is more significant than strength, and as long as ignition and carburettor have been set up properly, the bike should fire up promptly.

Electric starters should engage cleanly – if the starter doesn't engage and just whizzes over, it's likely that the sprag clutch has failed, which is expensive to put right. Unless the price is right, it's a reason to reject the bike, as there are plenty of Bullets around with working electric starts. EFIs, from cold, should start first time, using the cold start lever and no throttle.

There's a technique to starting, but it's not too difficult.

However it starts, the engine should settle down to a nice steady thump, thump idle. Uneven running and idling could be caused by air leaks between the carburettor and filter, which upsets the mixture. EFIs are generally reliable, though bad connections (the block connectors can corrode) and poor earths can upset idling and running. If the EFI warning light stays on after the engine has started, there is a fault somewhere in the system. This can be diagnosed by an Enfield dealer with the correct equipment.

Does the starter engage quickly and cleanly?

Engine – smoke/noise 4 3 2 1

If you're used to quiet, modern water-cooled engines, don't be alarmed by the merry tapping emanating from the Bullet's rocker boxes, as they all do that to an extent. EFI hydraulic tappets do tap for a few seconds from a cold start, but this should soon fade away. Adjusting the tappets on carburettor bikes is an easy enough job.

The Bullet's engine is basically strong, especially the understressed 350, and the EFI bottom end is strongest of all, but knocking or rumbling from the bottom end will mean a complete engine rebuild for sure. Whether it's big-ends or mains that need attention, the cure entails taking the engine out and completely stripping it down. Don't buy a bike that's making these noises unless it's cheap. Engine parts to cure all of this are no problem at all, for all bikes. The Sixty-5 and Electra X have a weakness in their roller bearing big-end – the rollers run directly in the bearing, and can fail, even today when the bikes are more than ten years old. The ultimate cure is an Alpha big-end, which is expensive but very strong. The plain big-end on iron-barrel 350s and 500s is less of a problem.

Now look back at the silencers and blip the throttle. Blue smoke means the engine is burning oil and is a sign of general wear in the top end, with pistons/rings and valves the culprits. That usually means a re-bore and again, parts, including oversize pistons, are available. Carburettor Bullets don't use a lot of oil and EFIs even less, so an engine in good condition shouldn't show any blue smoke.

Fuel-injection engines are less prone to leaks and neglect.

Not a Bullet, but the blue smoke suggests a worn top end.

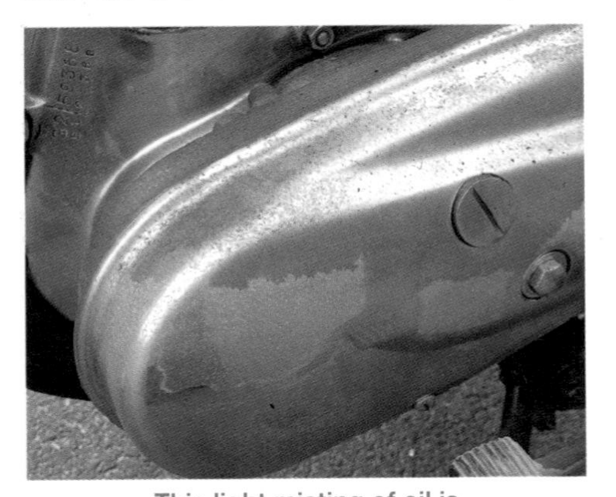
This light misting of oil is nothing to worry about.

Black smoke, indicating rich running, is less of a problem, caused by carburettor wear or (fingers crossed) simply a blocked air filter.

Bikes without air filters should be avoided, as you don't know what they've ingested over the years.

Take a general look – oil may be from leaks or the breather.

Primary drive

4 3 2 1

While the engine is running, listen for clonks or rumbles from the primary drive. There are no fundamental weaknesses here so we're looking out for general wear. Carburettor bikes have a primary chain adjuster, which may have been neglected, as you need to remove the chain cover to do the job – rattling could be nothing more scary than a loose chain. EFIs have an automatic chain adjuster, so there shouldn't be any rattles.

Noise from here suggests primary drive or clutch wear – chain on carburettor bikes can be adjusted manually.

Other noises could be clutch wear, the engine sprocket chattering on worn splines or the alternator rotor coming loose on the crank's driving shaft. Of course, you won't know which without taking the primary drive cover off, but if the seller acknowledges that a noise is there, it's another good lever to reduce the price.

Chain/sprockets

4 3 2 1

With the engine switched off, examine the final drive chain and sprockets. Is the chain clean, well lubed and properly adjusted? The best way to check how worn it is is to take hold of a link and try to pull it rearwards away from the sprocket. It should only reveal a small portion of the sprocket teeth – any more, and it needs replacing.

Check the rear sprocket teeth for wear – if they have a hooked appearance, the sprocket needs replacing. Ditto if any teeth are damaged or missing. And if the rear sprocket needs replacing, then the gearbox sprocket will too. Chain and sprockets aren't massively expensive, but changing the gearbox sprocket takes some dismantling time.

Check chain wear by pulling the chain rearwards.

Battery

4 3 2 1

Now check the battery, easily accessible behind the left-hand cover – a bolt-on steel box on carburettor bikes, a lockable plastic cover on the Electra X and all EFIs. If the battery is a top-up type, the correct electrolyte level is a good sign of a meticulous owner. Check that the battery is securely in place.

The battery is found under the left-hand cover on all bikes.

Engine/gearbox mountings

4 3 2 1

These need to be completely solid, with no cracks, and no missing or loose bolts – if not, the bike is not in a rideable condition.

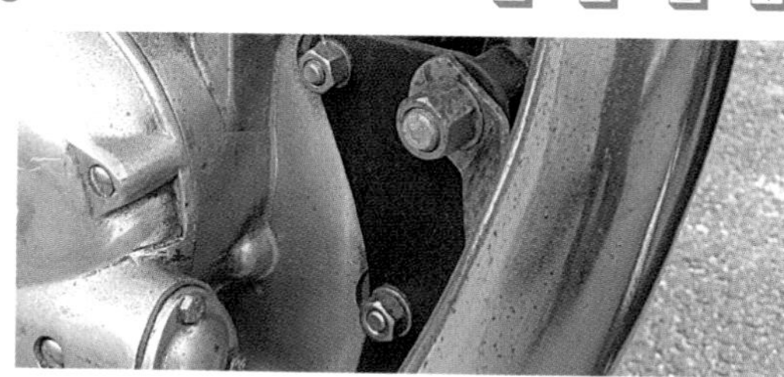

Are the engine mountings tight and secure?

Expect some bluing on exhaust downpipe chrome – it's barely discoloured on this low mileage GT.

Exhaust

4 3 2 1

Check that the downpipe is secure in the cylinder head, whether it's a push-fit or secured by a flange and bolts – looseness causes air leaks. Examine all joints for looseness and leaks, all of which are MoT failures. The silencer should be secure, firmly mounted and in solid condition. Replacements for all types are available. On EFIs some owners have replaced the original catalyst silencer with something louder and/or less restrictive. If the original exhaust comes with the bike, that's a bonus.

Bolted downpipe flange on a fuel-injection bike.

1993 silencer, pitted with rust but otherwise serviceable.

Test ride

The test ride should be not less than 10 minutes, and you should be doing the riding – not the seller riding with you on the pillion. It's understandable that some sellers are reluctant to let a complete stranger loose on their pride and joy, but it does go with the territory of selling a bike, and so long as you leave an article of faith (usually the vehicle you arrived in) then all should be happy. Take your driving licence in case the seller wants to see it.

There's no substitute for a test ride.

Warning lights 4 3 2 1

All bikes have main beam and indicator warning lights, either mounted in the speedo (later bikes) or in the nacelle (earlier ones). EFIs have a warning light for the injection system, which should come on for a few seconds when the ignition is turned on, and then go off.

Just two warning lights on early four-speed (main beam and indicators) – later speedo (shown) has lights incorporated.

If it stays on while the engine is running, there's a fault. All EFIs have a neutral light, and the GT also has a battery warning light, which should go out at a fast idle. If it stays on, the alternator isn't charging or the battery voltage is low.

GT warning lights.

Engine performance 4 3 2 1

If you haven't ridden an old British single before, the Bullet will seem slow and ponderous – remember that the 350 offers only 17bhp and the 500s 20-something. However, they should still pull cleanly and without hesitation – these bikes won't rev anything like as hard as a small modern bike, but are reasonably willing, and the GT's lighter crank does enable it to spin up slightly more quickly.

Low fuel and engine management warning lights on EFI (not GT).

On carburettor bikes, the difference between 350 and 500 performance isn't that great, though the 500 has more torque, and will pull more strongly at low/medium revs. It also has higher gearing, so will be more relaxed at a 50-60mph cruise. 350s should hold a 50-55mph cruise on the flat without a problem, and 500s should manage 55-60mph.

Some riders still prefer the 350, which isn't so prone to vibration, although there's also quite a difference between individual bikes – some are simply smoother than others, which is largely down to tolerances in crankshaft manufacture. Whichever bike it is, expect the vibes to come through over 50mph (maybe 60mph on EFIs), though these should be fairly mild – the bike shouldn't feel as if it's shaking itself to pieces.

The same comments apply to the EFIs, which should pull evenly through the rev range. Faults, usually down to poor connections, show up in misfiring, but are rare.

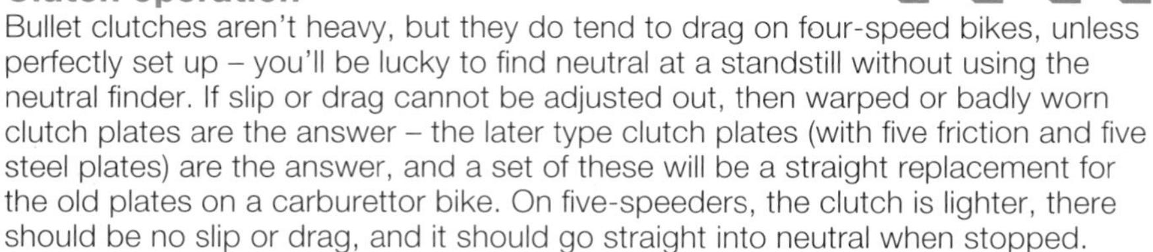

Clutch operation

4 3 2 1

Bullet clutches aren't heavy, but they do tend to drag on four-speed bikes, unless perfectly set up – you'll be lucky to find neutral at a standstill without using the neutral finder. If slip or drag cannot be adjusted out, then warped or badly worn clutch plates are the answer – the later type clutch plates (with five friction and five steel plates) are the answer, and a set of these will be a straight replacement for the old plates on a carburettor bike. On five-speeders, the clutch is lighter, there should be no slip or drag, and it should go straight into neutral when stopped.

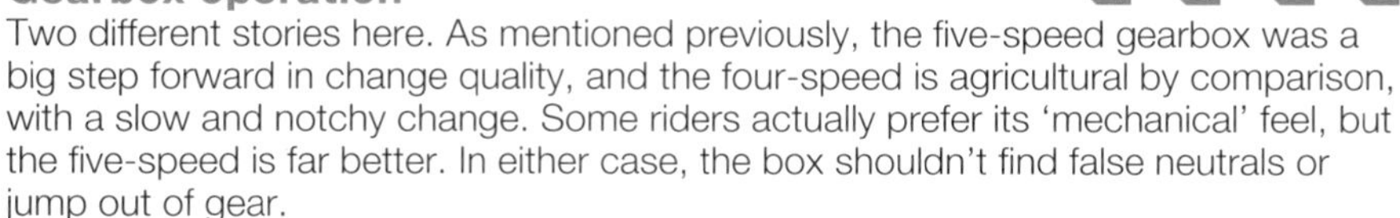

Gearbox operation

4 3 2 1

Two different stories here. As mentioned previously, the five-speed gearbox was a big step forward in change quality, and the four-speed is agricultural by comparison, with a slow and notchy change. Some riders actually prefer its 'mechanical' feel, but the five-speed is far better. In either case, the box shouldn't find false neutrals or jump out of gear.

Handling

4 3 2 1

Enfield Bullets are often seen as staid motorcycles, good only for pottering, but they actually handle quite well. These are relatively light bikes with stiff suspension, reasonably agile and fun on twisty roads. So any vagueness and weaving is usually down to worn forks, rear shocks or tyres – it's not inherent. They should never feel soft and wallowy – if they do, the suspension condition is your first thing to re-check. If the bike pulls to one side in a straight line, the wheels may be out of line.

A Bullet should handle well and pull cleanly.

Brakes

Braking varies from poor on the 350, with its six-inch single leading-shoe front drum, through to excellent on the 2012-on Bullets with Brembo front discs. The GT has always had Brembo discs front and rear.

Later Brembo discs are very good, but check calipers aren't sticking.

On drum brakes, if the lever or pedal oscillates, then that's a sign of an ovalled drum, which can only be cured by taking the brake apart and having the drum skimmed. Twin leading-shoe front drums, as on the early carburettor 500s, are variable – quite good with nicely round drums, and when set up correctly. In all cases, the rear drum brakes

6-inch rear drums are surprisingly powerful.

are pretty good. The discs and pads on EFIs wear well, but the cylinder will stick after a few years, especially if the bike has been used in all weathers and not been cleaned, or if it has sat for long periods unused.

Twin leading-shoe drum can work well if set up correctly.

Cables

4   

All the control cables – brakes, clutch, throttle, decompressor and choke/cold start – should work smoothly without stiffness or jerking. Poorly lubricated, badly adjusted cables are an indication of general neglect, and the same goes for badly routed cables.

Do all the cables operate smoothly?

Switchgear

Switchgear quality varies according to age. Early carburettor bikes have an unreliable light switch on the nacelle, though the German Magura handlebar switches used on 1990s export Bullets are very good – the Indian made Minda switches which replaced them aren't as positive. Best of the lot are the modern switches fitted to EFIs, which don't appear to have any common faults.

Whichever switches the bike has, just check that they work. Malfunctioning switches are usually a simple problem to solve, but another reason to bargain over price.

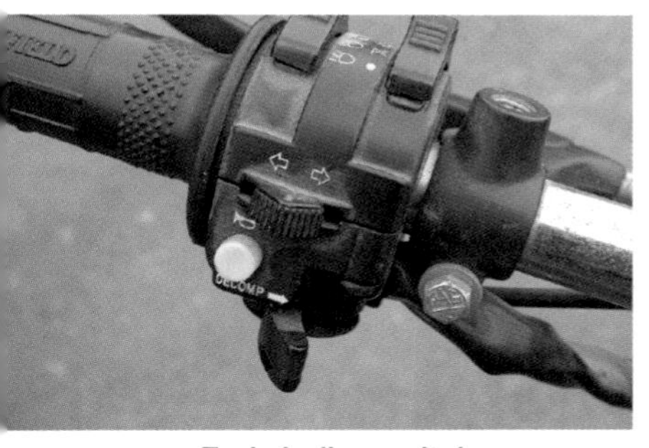

Early Indian switches are less robust.

Fuel-injection Bullets have good quality switches.

Evaluation procedure

Add up the total points.

Score: 128 = excellent; 96 = good; 64 = average; 32 = poor.

Bikes scoring over 90 will be completely usable and will require only maintenance and care to preserve condition. Bikes scoring between 32 and 65 will require some serious work (at much the same cost regardless of score). Bikes scoring between 66 and 89 will require very careful assessment of the necessary repair/restoration costs in order to arrive at a realistic value.

10 Auctions

– sold! Another way to buy your dream

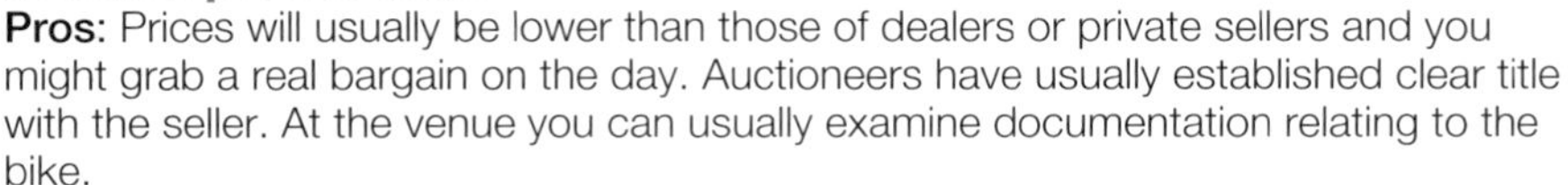

Auction pros & cons

Pros: Prices will usually be lower than those of dealers or private sellers and you might grab a real bargain on the day. Auctioneers have usually established clear title with the seller. At the venue you can usually examine documentation relating to the bike.

Cons: You have to rely on a sketchy catalogue description of condition & history. The opportunity to inspect is limited and you cannot ride the bike. Auction machines can be a little below par and may require some work. It's easy to overbid. There will usually be a buyer's premium to pay in addition to the auction hammer price.

Which auction?

Auctions by established auctioneers are advertised in the motorcycle magazines and on the auction houses' websites. A catalogue, or a simple printed list of the lots for auctions might only be available a day or two ahead, though often lots are listed and pictured on auctioneers' websites much earlier.

Ask the auction company if previous auction selling prices are available as this is useful information (details of past sales are often available on websites).

Catalogue, entry fee and payment details

When you purchase the catalogue of the bikes in the auction, it often acts as a ticket allowing two people to attend the viewing days and the auction. Catalogue details tend to be comparatively brief, but will include information such as 'one owner from new, low mileage, full service history', etc. It will also usually show a guide price to give you some idea of what to expect to pay and will tell you what is charged as a 'Buyer's premium'.

The catalogue will also contain details of acceptable forms of payment. At the fall of the hammer an immediate deposit is usually required, the balance payable within 24 hours. If the plan is to pay by cash there may be a cash limit. Some auctions will accept payment by debit card. Sometimes credit or charge cards are acceptable, but will often incur an extra charge. A bank draft or bank transfer will have to be arranged in advance with your own bank as well as with the auction house. No bike will be released before all payments are cleared. If delays occur in payment transfers then storage costs can accrue.

Buyer's premium

A buyer's premium will be added to the hammer price: don't forget this in your calculations. It is not usual for there to be a further state tax or local tax on the purchase price and/or on the buyer's premium.

Viewing

In some instances it's possible to view on the day or days before, as well as in the hours prior to, the auction. There are auction officials available who are willing to help out if need be. While the officials may start the engine for you, a test ride is out of the question. Crawling under and around the bike as much as you want is permitted. You can also ask to see any documentation available.

Bidding

Before you take part in the auction, **decide your maximum bid - and stick to it!**

It may take a while for the auctioneer to reach the lot you are interested in, so use that time to observe how other bidders behave. When it's the turn of your bike, attract the auctioneer's attention and make an early bid. The auctioneer will then look to you for a reaction every time another bid is made. Usually the bids will be in fixed increments until the bidding slows, when smaller increments will often be accepted before the hammer falls. If you want to withdraw from the bidding, make sure the auctioneer understands your intentions - a vigorous shake of the head when he or she looks to you for the next bid should do the trick!

Assuming that you are the successful bidder, the auctioneer will note your card or paddle number, and from that moment on you will be responsible for the bike.

If it is unsold, either because it failed to reach the reserve or because there was little interest, it may be possible to negotiate with the owner, via the auctioneers, after the sale is over.

Successful bid

There are two more items to think about - how to get the bike home, and insurance. If you can't ride it, your own or a hired trailer is one way, another is to have it shipped using the facilities of a local company. The auction house will also have details of companies specialising in the transport of bikes.

Insurance for immediate cover can usually be purchased on site, but it may be more cost-effective to make arrangements with your own insurance company in advance, and then call to confirm the full details.

eBay & other online auctions?

eBay & other online auctions once had a reputation for bargains. You could still land a Bullet at a bargain price, though many traders as well as private sellers now use eBay and prices have risen. As with any auction, the final price depends how many buyers are bidding and how desperately they want the bike!

Either way, it would be foolhardy to bid without examining the bike first, which is something most vendors encourage. A useful feature of eBay is that the geographical location of the bike is shown, so you can narrow your choices to those within a realistic radius of home. Be prepared to be outbid in the last few moments of the auction. Remember, your bid is binding and that it will be very, very difficult to get restitution in the case of a crooked vendor fleecing you - caveat emptor! Look at the seller's rating as well as the bike.

Be aware that some bikes offered for sale in online auctions are 'ghost' machines. Don't part with any cash without being sure that the vehicle does actually exist and is as described (usually pre-bidding inspection is possible).

Auctioneers

Bonhams: www.bonhams.com
British Car Auctions: (BCA) www.bca-europe.com or www.british-car-auctions.co.uk
Cheffins: www.cheffins.co.uk
eBay:www.ebay.co.uk or www.ebay.com
H&H: www.classic-auctions.co.uk
Shannons: www.shannons.com.au
Silver: www.silverauctions.com

11 Paperwork

– correct documentation is essential!

The paper trail

Older bikes sometimes come with a portfolio of paperwork accumulated by previous owners. This documentation represents the real history of the machine, from which you can deduce how well it's been cared for, how much it's been used, which specialists have worked on it and major repairs and restoration dates. This information will be priceless to you as the new owner, so be wary of bikes with little paperwork supporting a claimed history.

Registration documents

All countries/states have a form of registration for private vehicles, whether it's like the American 'pink slip' system or the British 'log book' system.

Check that the registration document is genuine, that it relates to the bike in question, and that all the details are correctly recorded, including frame and engine numbers (if shown). If you are buying from the previous owner, his or her name and address will be recorded in the document: this will not be the case if you are buying from a dealer.

In the UK the current (Euro-aligned) registration document is the V5C; printed in coloured sections of blue, green and pink. The blue section relates to the motorcycle specification, the green section has details of the registered keeper (who is not necessarily the legal owner) and the pink section is sent to the DVLA in the UK when the bike is sold. A small section in yellow deals with selling within the motor trade.

In the UK the DVLA will provide details of earlier keepers of the bike upon payment of a small fee, and much can be learned in this way.

If the bike has a foreign registration, there may be expensive and time-consuming formalities to complete. Do you really want the hassle? You'll need to re-register it, and of course, an Indian registered Bullet will be built to home market spec, not the better quality export specification.

Roadworthiness certificate

Most country/states require that bikes are regularly tested to prove that they are safe to use on the public highway. In the UK that test (the 'MoT') is carried out at approved testing stations, for a fee. In the USA, the requirement varies, but most states insist on an emissions test every two years as a minimum, while the police are charged with pulling over unsafe-looking vehicles.

In the UK the test is required on an annual basis for all post-1960 vehicles of more than three years old. Even if it isn't a legal necessity, a conscientious owner can opt to put the bike through the test anyway, as a health check. Of particular relevance for older bikes is that the certificate issued includes the mileage reading recorded at the test date and, therefore, becomes an independent record of that machine's history. Ask the seller if previous certificates are available. Without an MoT the bike should be trailered to its new home, unless you insist that a valid MoT is part of the deal. (Not such a bad idea this, as at least you will know the bike was roadworthy on the day it was tested and you don't need to wait for the old certificate to expire before having the test done.)

Road licence

The administration of every country/state charges some kind of tax for the use of its road system, the actual form of the 'road licence' and, how it is displayed, varying enormously country to country and state to state.

The road licence must relate to the vehicle carrying it and must be present and valid if the bike is to be ridden on the public highway legally. The value of the licence will depend on the length of time it will continue to be valid.

In the UK, if a bike is untaxed because it has not been used for a period of time, the owner has to inform the licencing authorities, otherwise the vehicle's date-related registration number will be lost and there will be a painful amount of paperwork to get it re-registered. Also, bikes built before 1st January 1976 are road tax exempt, which sadly doesn't apply to any of the Indian Enfield Bullets. They still had to display a valid paper disc until 1st October 2014, when these were abolished.

Certificates of authenticity

For many makes of older bike it is possible to get a certificate proving the age and authenticity (e.g. engine and frame numbers, paint colour and trim) of a particular machine. These are sometimes called 'Heritage Certificates' and if the bike comes with one of these it is a definite bonus. If you want to obtain one, the Royal Enfield Owners' Club is the best starting point.

Valuation certificate

A recent valuation certificate, or letter signed by a recognised expert stating how much they believe the particular bike to be worth, are usually needed to get 'agreed value' insurance. This applies more to older classic bikes. In any case, such documents should act only as confirmation of your own assessment of the bike rather than a guarantee of value, as the expert may not have seen it in the flesh. The easiest way to find out how to obtain a formal valuation is via the Owners' Club.

Service history

These bikes may have been serviced at home by enthusiastic (and hopefully capable) owners for a good number of years. Nevertheless, try to obtain as much service history and other paperwork pertaining to the bike as you can. Naturally, specialist garage receipts score most points in the value stakes. Anything helps in the great authenticity game, items like the original bill of sale, handbook, parts invoices and repair bills, adding to the story and the character of the machine. Even a brochure correct to the year of the bike's manufacture is a useful document and something that you could well have to search hard to locate in future years.

If the seller claims to have carried out regular servicing, ask what work was completed, when, and seek some evidence of it being carried out. Your assessment of the bike's overall condition should tell you whether the seller's claims are genuine.

Restoration photographs

If the seller tells you the bike has been restored, expect to be shown receipts and a series of photographs taken while the work was under way. Pictures taken at various stages, and from various angles, should help you gauge the thoroughness of the work. If you buy the bike, ask for copies of all the photographs as they form an important part of its history.

12 What's it worth?

– let your head rule your heart!

Condition

If the bike you've been looking at is really ratty, then you've probably not bothered to use the marking system in chapter 9 - 30 minute evaluation. You may not have even got as far as using that chapter at all!

If you did use the marking system in chapter 9 you'll know whether the bike is in Excellent (maybe Concours), Good, Average or Poor condition or, perhaps, somewhere between these categories.

To keep up to date with prices, buy the latest editions of the classic bike magazines and check the classified and dealer ads, both in the magazines and online – these are particularly useful as they enable you to compare private and dealer prices. Most of the magazines run auction reports as well, which publish the actual selling prices, as do the auction house websites. Remember that the price listed for online auctions (unless it's a 'Buy it Now' price) is only the highest current bid, not the final selling price.

Indian Enfield Bullets, because they are still in production and relatively plentiful, are not going up in value, though it looks likely that original four-speed 350s and 500s will begin to appreciate, as production has now stopped and they are becoming more sought after, even in India itself. The rarer UK specials from Watsonian and Hitchcocks do command a premium, and an Egli Bullet certainly will.

Assuming that the bike you have in mind is not in show/concours condition, then relate the level of condition that you judge it to be in with the appropriate price in the adverts. How does the figure compare with the asking price?

Before you start haggling with the seller, consider what affect any variation from standard specification might have on the bike's value. This is a personal thing: for some, absolute originality is non-negotiable, while others see non-standard parts as an opportunity to pick up a bargain. Do your research in the reference books, so that you know the bike's spec when it left the factory. That way, you shouldn't end up paying a top-dollar price for a non-original bike. If you are buying from a dealer, remember prices are generally higher than in private sales.

Striking a deal

Negotiate on the basis of your condition assessment, mileage, and fault rectification cost. Also take into account the bike's specification. Be realistic about the value, but don't be completely intractable: a small compromise on the part of the vendor or buyer will often facilitate a deal at little real cost.

13 Do you really want to restore?

– it'll take longer and cost more than you think

There's a romance about restoration projects, about bringing a sick bike back into blooming health, and it's tempting to buy something that 'just needs a few small jobs' to bring it up to scratch. But there are two things to think about: One, once you've got the bike home and start taking it apart, those few small jobs could turn into big ones. Secondly, restoration takes time, which is a precious thing in itself. Be honest with yourself – will you get as much pleasure from working on the bike as you will from riding it?

Restoration can be a messy business ...

Of course, you could hand over the whole lot to a professional, and the biggest cost involved there is not the new parts, but the sheer labour involved. Such restorations don't come cheap, and if taking this route there are four other issues to bear in mind.

First, make it absolutely clear what you want doing. Do you want the bike to be 100% original at the end of the process, or simply usable? Do you want a concours finish, or are you prepared to put up with a few blemishes on the original parts?

Second, make sure that not only is a detailed estimate involved, but that it is more or less binding. There are too many stories of a person quoted one figure only to be presented with an invoice for a far larger one!

Third, check that the company you're dealing with has a good reputation – the Owners' Club, or one of the reputable parts suppliers, should be able to make a few recommendations.

With all original paint and fittings, sometimes it's best to leave a bike unrestored.

A concours finish looks great, but won't be financially worthwhile.

Worth restoring? This1993 Bullet isn't cosmetically perfect, but rides well.

Finally, having an Indian Enfield Bullet professionally restored will not make financial sense as it's likely to cost more than the finished bike will be worth – not that this should put you off, if you have the budget, and really want to do it this way.

Restoring the bike yourself requires a number of skills, which is fine, if you already have them, but if you haven't it's good not to make your newly acquired bike part of the learning curve! Can you weld? Are you confident about building up an engine? Do you have a warm, well-lit garage with a solid workbench and good selection of tools?

Be prepared for a top-notch professional to put you on a lengthy waiting list, or, if tackling a restoration yourself, expect things to go wrong, and set aside extra time to complete the task. Restorations can stretch into years when things like life intrude, so it's good to have some sort of target date.

There's a lot to be said for a rolling restoration, especially as the summers start to pass with your Bullet still off the road. This is not the way to achieve a concours finish, which can only really be done via a thorough nut-and-bolt rebuild, without the bike getting wet and gritty in the meantime, but an 'on-the-go' restoration does have its plus points. Riding helps keep your interest as the bike's condition improves, and it's also more affordable than trying to do everything in one go. In the long run, it will take longer, but you'll get some on-road fun out of the bike in the meantime.

14 Paint problems

– a bad complexion, including dimples, pimples and bubbles ...

Paint faults generally occur due to lack of protection/maintenance, or to poor preparation prior to a respray or touch-up. Some of the following conditions may be present in the bike you're looking at:

Orange peel

This appears as an uneven paint surface, similar to the appearance of the skin of an orange. The fault is caused by the failure of atomised paint droplets to flow into each other when they hit the surface. It's sometimes possible to rub out the effect with proprietary paint cutting/rubbing compound or very fine grades of abrasive paper. A respray may be necessary in severe cases. Consult a paint shop for advice.

Cracking

Severe cases are likely to have been caused by too heavy an application of paint (or filler beneath the paint). Also, insufficient stirring of the paint before application can lead to the components being improperly mixed, and cracking can result. Incompatibility with the paint already on the panel can have a similar effect. To rectify, it is necessary to rub down to a smooth, sound finish before respraying the problem area.

Crazing

Sometimes the paint takes on a crazed rather than a cracked appearance when the problems mentioned under 'cracking' are present. This problem can also be

Faded paint after 23 years on the road, but it really just needs a good clean.

caused by a reaction between the underlying surface and the paint. Paint removal and respraying is usually the only solution.

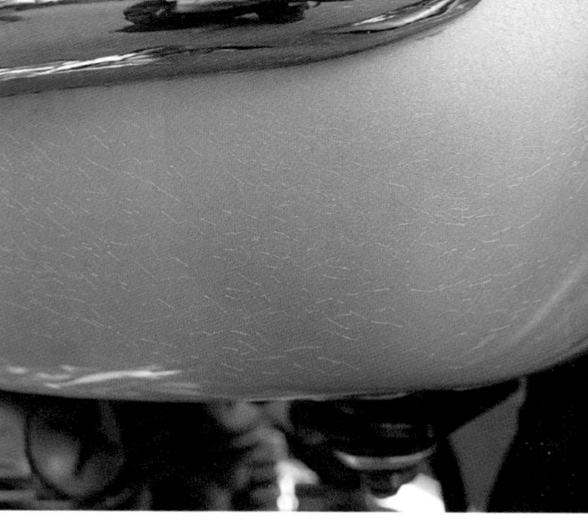

Crazed finish, curable by a respray only.

Blistering

Almost always caused by corrosion of the metal beneath the paint. Usually, perforation will be found in the metal, and the damage will often be worse than that suggested by the area of blistering. The metal will have to be repaired before repainting.

Micro blistering

Usually the result of an economy respray where inadequate heating has allowed moisture to settle on the vehicle before spraying. Consult a paint specialist, but damaged paint will have to be removed before partial or full respraying. Can also be caused by bike covers that don't 'breathe.'

Fading

Some colours, especially reds, are prone to fading if subject to strong sunlight for long periods without the benefit of polish protection. Sometimes proprietary paint restorers and/or paint cutting/rubbing compounds will retrieve the situation. Often a respray is the only real solution.

Peeling

Often a problem with metallic paintwork when the sealing lacquer becomes damaged and begins to peel off. Poorly applied paint may also peel. The remedy is to strip and start again.

Dimples

Dimples in the paintwork are caused by the residue of polish (particularly silicone types) not being removed properly before respraying. Paint removal and repainting is the only solution.

Petrol stains should polish out.

15 Problems due to lack of use

– just like their owners, Bullets need exercise!

Like any piece of engineering, and indeed like human beings, Enfield Bullets deteriorate if they sit doing nothing for long periods. This is especially relevant if the bike is laid up for six months of the year, as some are.

Rust

If the bike is put away wet, and/or stored a cold, damp garage, the paint, metal and brightwork will suffer. Ensure the machine is completely dry and clean before going into storage, and spray with an anti-corrosion oil. If you can afford it, invest in a dehumidifier to keep the atmosphere dry.

Damp storage leads to rust.

Cables

Cables are vulnerable to seizure – the answer is to thoroughly lube them beforehand, and come into the garage to give them a couple of pulls once a week or so.

Give the levers a pull once a week.

Tyres

If the bike's been left on its sidestand, most of its weight is on the tyres, which will develop flat spots and cracks over time. Always leave the bike on its centre stand.

Engine

Old, acidic oil can corrode bearings. Many riders change the oil in the spring, when they're putting the bike back on the road, but really it should be changed just before the bike is laid up, so that the bearings are sitting in fresh oil. The same goes for the gearbox. While you're giving the cables their weekly exercise, turn over the engine slowly on the kickstart, ignition off. Don't start it though – running the engine for a short time does more harm than good, as it produces a lot of moisture internally, which the engine doesn't get hot enough to burn off. That will attack the engine internals and the silencers.

Change the oil when the bike is put away.

Battery/electrics

Remove the battery and give it a top-up charge every couple of weeks, or connect it to a battery top-up device, such as the Optimate, which will keep it permanently fully charged. Damp conditions will allow fuses and earth connections to corrode, storing up electrical troubles for later. Eventually, wiring insulation will harden and fail.

16 The Community

– key people, organisations and companies in the Bullet world

Manufacturer

Royal Enfield
www.royalenfield.com

Auctioneers

See chapter 10

Clubs across the world

Royal Enfield Owners' Club – UK
www.royalenfield.org.uk

Royal Enfield Owners' Club – France
Marylene Martin
0033 1600 28417

Royal Enfield Owners' Club – Germany
www.reoc.de

Royal Enfield Owners' Club - Greece
Email: koncharalamb@yahoo.gr or andrew-pap@hotmail.com
Facebook: www.facebook.com/groups/591037007731075/

Royal Enfield Owners' Club – Finland
Email: reoc.finland@yahoo.co.uk

Royal Enfield Owners' Club – North America
Email: dalec@ar51.net

Royal Enfield Club of Australia
www.recoainc.com

New Zealand Royal Enfield Register
www.royalenfield.org.nz

Royal Enfield Owners' Italia – Italy
www.facebook.com/Royal-Enfield-Owners-Italia-241045265947925/

Royal Indians – India
www.royalindians.com

Royal Enfield Owners' Club – South Africa
www.facebook.com/REsouthafrica

Specialists

We have restricted our listing to UK companies. This list does not imply recommendation and is not deemed to be comprehensive.

Hitchcocks Motorcycles
www.hitchcocksmotorcycles.com

Price Parts Motorcycles
www.pricepartmotorcycles.co.uk

The Bullet-In
www.thebullet-in.com

Watsonian-Squire (sidecars)
www.watsonian-squire.com

Electrex World (ignition/electrical parts)
www.electrexworld.co.uk
01491 682369

Books

Royal Enfield books
Books, workshop manuals and parts books
www.royalenfieldbooks.com

Made in India – The Royal Enfield Bullet
Gordon May
RG Publishing 2014

Royal Enfield, the Complete Story
(mostly covers UK-built bikes)
Mick Walker
Crowood Press 2003

17 Vital statistics

– essential data at your fingertips

Listing the vital statistics of every Bullet variant would take more room than we have here, so we've picked three representative models: 1978 350 Standard; 2004 Electra X; 2015 Continental GT.

	1978 350 Standard	2004 500 Electra X	GT
Max speed	70mph approx	75mph approx	85mph approx
Engine	Air-cooled OHV single – 346cc Bore and stroke 70 x 90mm. Compression ratio 6.5:1. Power: 18bhp @ 5625rpm	Air-cooled OHV single – 499cc Bore and stroke 84 x 90mm. Compression ratio 8.5:1. Power: 23bhp @ 5500rpm	Air-cooled OHV single – 535cc Bore and stroke 87 x 90mm. Compression ratio 8.5:1. Power: 29bhp @ 5100rpm.
Gearbox	Four-speed. Ratios: 1st 2.77:1, 2nd 1.84:1, 3rd 1.36:1, 4th 1.0:1.	Five-speed. Ratios: 1st 3.06:1, 2nd 2.01:1, 3rd 1.52:1, 4th 1.21:1, 5th 1.0:1	Five-speed. Ratios: 1st 3.06:1, 2nd 2.01:1, 3rd 1.52:1, 4th 1.21:1, 5th 1.0:1.
Brakes	6in SLS drums front and rear.	Front disc, rear 6in drum.	Front 300mm disc, rear 240mm disc.
Electrics	6-volt	12-volt	12-volt
Weight	358lb/162kg.	370lb/168kg.	405lb/184kg.

Bullet timeline

1977: Bullet first imported to the UK by Slater Bros.
1983: Tank badges change from 'Enfield India' to 'Enfield'.
1986: Bullets now EC/DOT approved for import. Twelve-volt electrics.
1987: Superstar launched, Mikarb replaces Bing.
1988: Bullet 500 launched, with 22bhp and 7in TLS front brake.
1989: Stepped seat on export bikes.
1992: Horn now front facing.
1993: Folding kickstart, warning lights inside speedometer.
1994: Eicher takes over Royal Enfield, quality improves. Ignition switch moves to nacelle, light switch to left-hand handlebar.
1995: Lockable toolbox.
1996: Pulse Air Valve emissions control on 500.
1997: Tank badge changes to 'Royal Enfield' from 'Enfield'.
1998: Crankcase breather feeds back into crankcase (export bikes), wiring block connectors replace bullet connects, shielded wheel bearings.
1999: Watsonian new UK importer, 'Royal Enfield' logo on all rubber parts.
2000: Clubman 500S launched, crankcase fastenings now metric.
2001: Electric start ES launched, integral steering lock.
2003: 5-speed Sixty-5 launched, screw type dipstick.
2004: Electra X launched.
2007: Woodsman special launched by Watsonian.
2009: EFI launched in Electra and Classic forms.
2011: B5 EFI launched.
2012: MotoGB new UK importer, Thunderbird 500 launched (not for UK), Bullet Satin launched.
2013: GT launched.

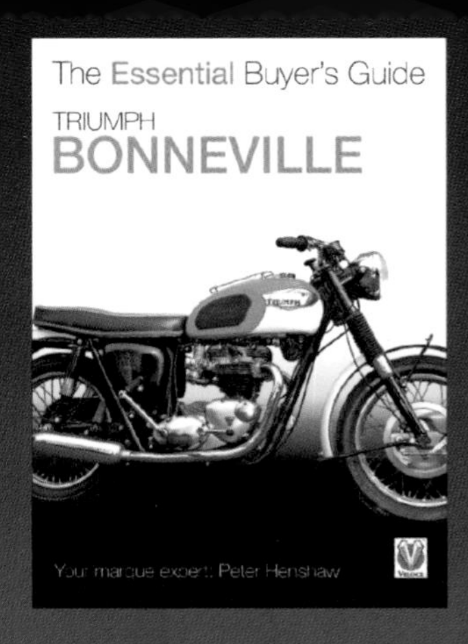

ISBN: 978-1-84584-134-8
£9.99* UK/$19.95* USA

ISBN: 978-1-845842-81-9
£12.99* UK/$25* USA

ISBN: 978-1-845849-41-2
£12.99* UK/$25* USA

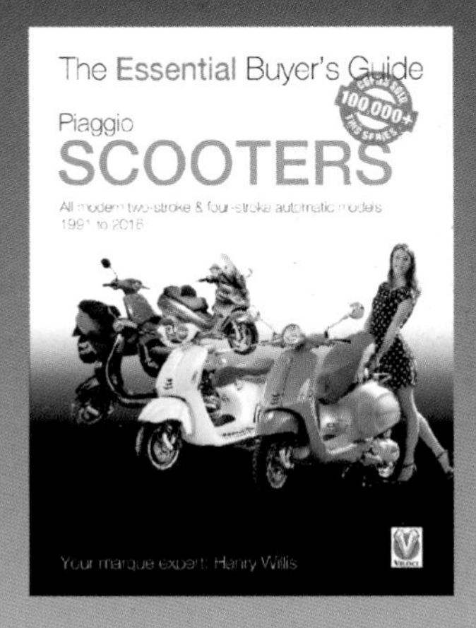

ISBN: 978-1-845849-92-4
£12.99* UK/$25* USA

Having these books in your pocket is like having a real marque expert by your side. Benefit from the authors' years of real ownership experience, learn how to spot a bad car quickly, and how to assess a promising one like a professional. Get the right car at the right price!

* prices subject to change, p&p extra

The Essential Buyer's Guide™ series ...

978-1-845840-22-8

978-1-845840-26-6

978-1-845840-29-7

978-1-845840-77-8

978-1-845840-99-0

978-1-904788-70-6

978-1-845841-01-0

978-1-845841-07-2

978-1-845841-19-5

978-1-845841-13-3

978-1-845841-35-5

978-1-845841-36-2

978-1-845841-38-6

978-1-845841-46-1

978-1-845841-47-8

978-1-845841-61-4

978-1-845841-63-8

978-1-845841-65-2

978-1-845841-88-1

978-1-845841-92-8

978-1-845842-00-0

978-1-845842-04-8

978-1-845842-05-5

978-1-845842-31-4

978-1-845842-70-3

978-1-845842-81-9

978-1-845842-83-3

978-1-845842-84-0

978-1-845842-87-1

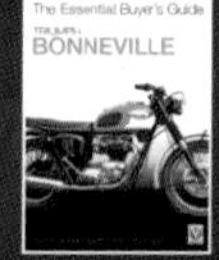

978-1-84584-134-8

978-1-845843-03-8

978-1-845843-07-6

978-1-845843-09-0

978-1-845843-16-8

978-1-845843-29-8

978-1-845843-30-4

978-1-845843-34-2

978-1-845843-38-0

978-1-845843-39-7

978-1-845843-40-3

£9.99 – £12.99 / $19.95 (prices subject to change, p&p extra)